They look so lovely when they're asleep

For
Jo and Bob
and Ilana
with lots of love
Diane

They look so lovely when they're asleep

Advice and anecdotes for practising parents

Diane Levy

RANDOM HOUSE
NEW ZEALAND

To all our grandchildren,
present and future
(No pressure, kids!)

New Zealand Cataloguing-in-Publication Data

Levy, Diane
They look so lovely when they're asleep:
advice and anecdotes for practising parents / Diane Levy
ISBN 1-8694-659-7
1. Parent and child. 2. Child rearing. I. Title
649.1-dc 22

A RANDOM HOUSE BOOK
published by
Random House New Zealand
18 Poland Road, Glenfield, Auckland, New Zealand
www.randomhouse.co.nz

First published 2004

© 2004 Diane Levy

The moral rights of the author have been asserted

ISBN 1 86941 659 7

Design: Kate Greenaway
Cover illustration and design: Vasanti Unka
Printed in Australia by Griffin Press

Contents

The title of this book   9
First things first — the purpose of this book   11

From *East & Bays Courier*

It's a tough job   13
Power-dressing for mothers   15
Is there a plan?   17
What is your parenting culture?   19
A winter's tale   21
The great plot   23
Living in a war zone   25
The seven-year itch   27
Kiss it better, Mummy   29
Raising good problem-solvers   31
Limited choice   33
Baby talk and phone talk   35
Reflecting the real world   37
Let's not tell the first fib   39
I wish I knew *the* parenting trick . . .   41
It's concert time again   43
It must be Christmas   45
Sorry kids! I've got all the time in the world   47
Sandcastles   49
Did I really need to shout so loud?   51
The new school year   53
Building a cathedral   56

Showing off is so very hard to do	58
Reading rooms	61
Different paths	63
The joys of mastery	65
Running away	68
Let's be civil	70
Grizzling is great	72
Pocket money	74
Memory training	76

From *Littlies*

Let's take time out	78
Let's avoid food wars	82
Night-time waking	86
Do tell tales	90
Is smacking the answer?	93
Building self-esteem in toddlers	96
Disciplining other people's children	100
Bribes, incentives and rewards	104
Sibling mayhem	108
Coping with trauma, loss and grief	112
Don't go, Mummy	116
Managing tantrums	120

From *Parenting With Confidence*

Fun and games	124
Making sure that fun really *is* fun for everyone	126
Shy children	129
Getting our children to do as they are told	133
When your child is being bullied	140

From *Fitness Life — Kids Life*

    Oh no! Mum's on another health kick!   144

From *Essentially Food*

    Supporting children when they are upset   148
    Peaceful holidays   154
    It's never too late to set up routines   157
    Toddler-proofing your baby   162
    What is pocket money for?   165
    After-school activities   169
    The rain dance   173
    You can't go out looking like that!   176
    Family meals — heaven or hell?   178
    Show some respect   182
    C U L8R! GR8!   186

The title of this book

LET'S START AT THE very beginning — the title of this book. It all began with a poem.

FOR ALL US PARENTS . . . PAYBACK TIME

When I'm an old lady, I'll live with each kid,
And bring so much happiness . . . Just as they did.
I want to pay back all the joy they've provided,
Returning each deed – Oh, they'll be so excited!
When I'm an old lady and live with my kids.

I'll write on the walls, with reds, whites and blues.
I'll bounce on the furniture, wearing my shoes.
I'll drink from the carton and then leave it out.
I'll stuff all the toilets and Oh, how they'll shout!
When I'm an old lady and live with my kids.

When they're on the phone and just out of reach,
I'll get into things, like sugar and bleach.
They'll snap their fingers and then shake their head.
And when that is done, I'll hide under the bed!
When I'm an old lady and live with my kids.

When they cook dinner and call me to eat,
I'll not eat the green beans or salad or meat.
I'll gag on my spinach, spill milk on the table,
And when they get angry, I'll run . . . if I'm able!
When I'm an old lady and live with my kids.

I'll sit close to the TV, through channels I'll click,
I'll cross both my eyes just to see if they'll stick.
I'll take off my socks and throw one away,
And play in the mud till the end of the day!
When I'm an old lady and live with my kids.

And later in bed, I'll lie back and sigh,
I'll thank God in prayer and then close my eyes.
My kids will look down with a smile slowly creeping,
And say with a smile . . . 'She's so sweet when she's sleeping!'

I wish I could acknowledge and thank the source for this poem. As with so many things, both good and bad – 'it came off the internet!' I really related to the contents and, predictably, laughed out loud at the final line.

Hence the title of this book, *They look so lovely when they're asleep.*

First things first — the purpose of this book

IT IS MUCH MORE THAN A DECADE since I wrote my first magazine article. Since then, I have had the privilege of being invited to do three long-running series — with *East and Bays Courier*, *Essentially Food* and *Littlies* (a wonderful free magazine for practical parenting) — as well as sporadic articles for *Parenting with Confidence* and an article for the first edition of *Kids Life*.

The life of any magazine article is relatively short and I always had in mind, since the feedback was so wonderfully heartwarming, that there would come a time when I would make the articles available in a book.

This book of articles has four purposes for you, the reader. First, there are books of fiction, non-fiction, romance, journeys, thrillers, information, education, humour and pathos. (Come to think of it, the adventure of parenting includes all of these aspects.) However, although there are many parenting books of the 'how-to' variety, there are comparatively few books written about the day-to-day highs, lows and relentless in-betweens that we all go through as parents. So my first aim is that you enjoy the anecdotes and remember your childhood, your children's childhood, your grandchildren's childhood and the wonderful quirky things that children say and do.

Second, as current parents, we rarely have the time or the concentration to read a whole book or, speaking as an exhausted parent, to remember what it was we read the previous day and to pick up the theme twenty-four hours later. So this book is designed for the parent who needs a three-minute read (i.e. one short article) because that is all the time available.

Third, as well as entertaining anecdotes, there are many articles devoted to giving you good parenting tips and strategies.

Fourth, in my experience there is usually only one dedicated self-improver in the family. There is usually only one of us who pours over parenting books, looking for information, relief and solutions. Then we try to persuade our significant other to 'just read this bit'. They, the dedicated non-self-improver, promise to try and somehow never quite get around to it. I think this book will improve your chances. Put a book mark at the article you most want them to read, suggest 'Just read this one', and place the book in the place of most-likely reading, probably the bathroom!

So, I leave you to enjoy these articles in as little or as much time as you have.

It's a tough job

. . . BUT SOMEBODY'S GOT TO do it. I am talking about 'getting the show on the road'. This is the job with which most Household Managers, who can be identified by their unfailing response to the call of 'Mu-u-um', begin their day.

It is our job to get everyone out the door, dressed and fed, lunchbox in hand, homework done, clothes clean — and, so we don't have to face it later in the day — beds made and all signs of breakfast somehow miraculously disappeared.

This task does not stop at the letterbox, however. The Job Description includes getting everyone, or enabling everyone to get, to their destination. And some clown included in our Job Description 'It is your responsibility that everyone should get to their destination HAPPY. If not, your job may not be well done.'

And be warned. If you do this Job well once, it somehow becomes an appointment for life, a life-sentence.

I often ask myself how I landed this Job. I read time management books and they advised me to make a list of tomorrow's tasks. I prioritised them. I put the toughest one first. Bingo. I tried to delegate but discovered no one willing to be delegated to. And so it became all mine.

I have tried doing it badly, but the family just wait optimistically and patiently for me to remember how to get it right. I've tried shouting a lot — no effort required there, my volume button has been stuck since our first-born crawled — but they just whisper 'PMT' behind my back and wait for tomorrow.

It would appear that the only choice I have — and that is on the odd good day, the sort of day when I believe I have a choice — is to do it badly, or to do it well. So next time I'll talk to you about power-dressing for The Job.

— East & Bays Courier

Power-dressing for mothers

I'VE ALWAYS WONDERED HOW teachers manage. When they ask my child to sit on the mat, it never occurs to her to climb onto the kitchen bench. When they ask her to tidy up the block corner, she not only puts all the blocks away in their correct places according to size and shape, she even races to get it done quickly and then asks if there is anything else she can help with. And this from a child who, at home, can scarcely raise the motivation to put two books on her shelf without her mother resorting to dire threats.

I have finally discovered the teacher's secret. *She gets dressed before she goes to work!* By the time she greets my child, she is fully clothed, has combed her hair, cleaned her teeth, and has her eyes wide open. No wonder they take notice of her.

Contrast this scene. I stagger out of bed in a nightie named 'Old Faithful'. Pretending great joy at the blessings another day may have to offer, I shamble into the children's room saying 'Wake up, darling, time to get dressed', and, under an illusion completely unaffected by years of experience to the contrary, imagine that my children understand this to mean 'Get out of bed, get dressed, pack your bag and appear cheerfully for breakfast'.

When I return ten minutes later, clad in a damp towel and a few soap-flakes, no one has moved. Clearly shouting is the answer, so I do, causing the recipient to bury deep into the protective covers.

Mustering as much dignity as semi-nakedness allows, I noisily throw all the bedclothes on the floor. I must have done this many times, because my children are so skilled that they can get under the bedclothes before they (the blankets) hit the ground. The day goes steadily downhill from here.

There is a solution. It is called Power Dressing.

Get up a quarter of an hour before them. Be showered, dressed and ready. Then you can control your day — and the start of theirs. You can set the tone, be the example, be in charge.

Every time I begin my day this way, it works. It's just that steeling myself to do it is so hard. I think I can manage to try again next Thursday.

— East & Bays Courier

Is there a plan?

OR SHALL WE JUST play the whole thing by ear? Do we have a clearly defined set of goals, or are we doing Management by Crisis? Do we have a Mission Statement, or is 'Let's try to get through till 10.00 a.m. without one of us crying' about as good as it gets?

Luckily we don't stop to ask ourselves 'What is my Mission and what are my Goals?' until we are well into The Job. If we all *did* ask this question before we had children, it would be so overwhelming that there would be no contraceptive worries and no world population crisis!

However, if we *are* going to spend twenty years in one Job, or several contemporaneous Jobs, it would be a good idea to have some idea of what we are trying to achieve. In other words, a Mission Statement is called for and a Game Plan to achieve the Goals.

Richard Gordon, who wrote the 'Doctor in the House' series, described a newborn baby as 'a very short person with no discipline at either end'. It is our task to take these short persons and gradually transform them from unskilled to skilled, from dependent to independent, from undisciplined to self-disciplined, from amoral to moral, from a self-centred individual to a member of a couple, a family and a community.

And it is important to remember, there *are* compensations. The good thing about this Job — and it is important to cling to the hope that there is something good about it, because it surely isn't the conditions, the rates of pay, the hours, the sick leave, the tedium, the complete absence of maternity or paternity leave, the Super Scheme, and definitely not the holidays — is that the training is in-house and mistakes can be made in private. There exists the possibility of enormous job satisfaction. And — it is very hard to get fired.

— East & Bays Courier

What is your parenting culture?

I HAVE BEEN STRUGGLING with an explanation for the increase in the number and proportion of strong-willed, strong-minded, difficult-to-manage children that you can find in any family, crèche, pre-school or school. Both parents and teachers find themselves bewildered at the power that these children can exercise over both adults and other children.

I believe that the reason, for the majority of New Zealand families, is that we have no clear Parenting Culture. The cure lies in parents defining what that culture is for them and then training their children in the ways of their family's culture.

The dictionary defines 'culture' as 'the experimental growth of micro-organisms in a nutrient substance'. Provided you are prepared to extend the definition of micro-organisms to mean *small, live beings,* or *mean,* small live beings, as the case may be, it certainly is relevant.

Another definition of 'culture' is 'the total of ideas, beliefs, value and knowledge, which constitute the shared bases of social interaction.'

Put in a way that we can understand and use:

- As parents, it is our responsibility to set up rules and guidelines for our children.
- Until *we* know what our rules are, we cannot hope to teach them to our children.

- Our children have the right to know what the rules are and to be reasonably certain that their parents will uphold them most of the time.

So when we encounter misery, belligerence, rage or confusion in our children, the first question we need to ask ourselves is 'What is my Parenting Culture telling me to do in this situation?'

If the answer is 'Well, I could cuddle her, or I should send her to her room, or I might plonk her in front of the TV, or I should help her solve this, or she should be able to solve it herself, or she really needs a sleep, or it's probably the orange cordial, or I wonder if she is sickening for something, or I really can't stand this anymore and are there boarding schools for four year olds?' Congratulations! You qualify for The Normal Parents' Award.

That's the explanation. However, if you are after a solution, a way of handling the situation successfully, the first thing you need is clarity of purpose, your Parenting Culture. In other words, WHAT IS THE RULE? Because if you don't know what it is, if you couldn't write it down in one short sentence, it is impossible for your child to follow it.

It is that simple and that difficult.

— East & Bays Courier

A winter's tale

ON THE FIRST MORNING of the really cold snap, Deborah, aged nine, refused to get out of bed because it was too cold. Having been dragged out, she refused to get dressed because it was too cold. It plunged me right back to the winter of '68.

It's a good thing that Vernon and I were married in January. This meant that, by the time winter came around, our marriage was strong enough to survive a major disagreement about the best way to get out of bed in the morning.

I subscribed to the unshakeable belief that I should wake up about quarter of an hour before get-up time, turn the electric blanket on high so that, by the time my back was starting to get crisp, I had accumulated enough heat to leap out of bed, into a shower, into clothes, before my body had cooled down to a simmer. Thus, I was warm and ready to face the day.

Vernon was of much stronger mettle than this. He believed that the most helpful thing that he could do for me was to turn off the electric blanket, pull all my non-electric blankets (we were married so long ago that people still had blankets and only ducks slept under feathers) out of reach, preferably on the floor. The theory was that, if my bed was cold, I would get out and, once standing next to a pile of blankets on the other side of the room, would not consider it worth my while to get back in the bed.

Hence, 'Cool Mum' was known in our household way before we even contemplated 'Cool Kids.' His system did not work for us because Cool Mum instantaneously turned into Extremely Nasty When Freezing Person.

We resolved this, as with most of our disagreements, with the Fair Fighting Resolution for People Who Want a Long Term Relationship Method that we have been using since then. I get out of bed my way and Vernon gets out of bed his way.

As with most couple differences, this works very well until you have children and read a parenting book that says parents should be in agreement over important issues. Whose method of getting out of bed was going to predominate?

We had been tough on our first two children. No electric blankets. So getting out of a freezing room made getting into eventually warm clothing a comparative pleasure. The first two are the children we have raised.

Our last child is not for raising. She's for pleasure. And we have finally reached Parental Agreement. I agree that she shouldn't have an electric blanket, and Vernon agrees that she has four extra blankets and a hot water bottle. Deborah agrees that she gets out of bed in the morning feeling warm.

— *East & Bays Courier*

The great plot

MANY PEOPLE BELIEVE THAT there is The Great Plan and that an important part of our lives is to find out what our part should be in this Plan. I, however, believe that we are victims of The Great Plot.

The first part of The Plot is that Opposites Attract. You would think we would choose our life partners — a politically correct term for husbands or wives — on the basis that we see things the same way, we enjoy doing the same things, and have life goals and philosophies in common. But No. Strong-minded, goal-oriented people tend to marry phlegmatic, easy-going partners. Fun-loving, noisy, cheerful party animals tend to marry reserved people who need lots of space and silence.

Opposites do attract. Together we make up a complementary, and even a complimentary, team. Together we can face the world. Music plays. Bells chime. And, celebrating our differences, we walk hand-in-hand to face the future.

A few years of being just-the-two-of-us is really useful to learn how to accommodate these differences under one roof. When we have finally learned how to make our lives happy and fulfilling together, you'd think that the sensible thing to do would be to stop and enjoy. But no. We can't leave well enough alone, can we? We decide to have children. Believe it or not, we do not do this out of some evil masochistic inclination, but in the belief that it will enhance our relationship.

This is where The Great Plot really kicks in. We've just learned how to live with the first set of rules, Opposites Attract, and The Great Plot changes the Game Plan. From the moment our first born utters the first shriek, we become parents and, according to the rules, 'Parents Should Pull Together' and 'Speak With One Voice'.

It's enough to give anyone, male or female, post-natal depression. Overnight, we are expected to know what is on our partner's mind on every topic from 'the best way to burp the baby' to 'the best way to stop a teenager from burping in public' and to have reached agreement prior to knowing what the potential topic of disagreement might be.

It is not as though there is any time for discussion, even assuming two opposites could reach agreement. While your two-seconds-ago-perfectly-charming two-year-old has just hurled themselves on the ground in a raging tantrum in the middle of a busy mall, it scarcely seems appropriate to hold a Family Conference. 'I think the kid just needs a bit of control.' 'Well, *I* think the child is dreadfully upset.'

Perhaps the purpose of The Great Plot is to give our children the opportunity to Play it Down the Middle, Hone Their Negotiating Skills and Side with the Best Chance. It certainly seems designed that way.

— East & Bays Courier

Living in a war zone

THERE ARE TIMES WHEN our homes become a War Zone. We are minding our own business, working away, when we hear the rising tide of battle.

It begins gently enough. We hear sounds of negotiations in progress. Early clues to this procedure are words like 'It's mine'. 'No. It's mine'. 'Well I had it first'. This is a good time for Parental Deafness.

Unfortunately, our children know all about Parental Deafness and set about helping us. Because they love us so much, they compete strenuously with each other to see who can be the most helpful. The system they use is called Increase the Volume. We do not have to move one inch from where we are, because they, only in the interests of helping — of course, will raise the volume to such a pitch that we can hear every nuance of their negotiations from the furthest end of the house. How kind.

Sometimes Parental Deafness is so great that they become even more considerate. They understand how exhausting parenthood can be. So, they send a Messenger from the Front. 'She swiped my truck', 'He's being mean', and 'I didn't start it' are fairly common Strategic Messages.

Since we wish to teach our children independence and advanced negotiating skills, we offer profound advice like 'M-m-m-m-m' or 'I see'. The Messenger is enchanted with our simple-yet-kindly wisdom and races back to the Front. Somewhere, on the way down the corridor, they appoint themselves as Official Military Translator. The message therefore arrives in a different form. 'Mum says you've got to give it back — or else'. Should the recipient be a little slow to understand, the Translator can always elaborate on the message. 'You're really in for it now.'

A wise parent develops a new symptom — Lameness. This is also known as the inability to walk to the War Zone. Since threats were not enough, the protagonists have to use weaponry. Missiles begin to fly, at first falling in harmless places, eventually beginning to find their mark.

It is time for the Parental UN Observer to go in. We stroll, lameness now bravely overcome, down the corridor. We pause, powerfully, in the doorway and observe the instant cease-fire. Looking only mildly disapproving, we make a profound, yet completely neutral observation. 'This isn't working.'

While they hold their fire, stunned at our perspicacity, we quickly follow up with 'You go to your room and you go to your room. You can come out in ten minutes. I'll set the timer'.

Upon release, they have cooled down, forgotten the original cause of War, and are ready to join forces to outwit the Common Enemy. Guess Who?

They have also learned a very valuable lesson. Don't fight, or, if you must, do it very quietly so that Mum doesn't find out. Either way, who cares? Our mission is complete. We return to base.

Since our children are aware that we are slow learners, they are willing to help us by repeating the Battle many times so we get a chance to become really proficient observers. How kind.

— *East & Bays Courier*

The seven-year itch

THERE USED TO BE a saying about the 'Seven-Year Itch', implying that, every seven years, spouses became bored or irritated with one another. They would look around the home and think, 'Why am I putting up with this?' and then look outside the home and find greater attraction there.

I have my own theory about this. Every seven years or so, all the family electrical appliances begin to break down or wear out. Since it all happens in the same fortnight, the stress on the previously Cool Mum is enormous. What with finding diverse people to visit or receive the appliance, and then waiting with dismembered appliances for exotic parts to arrive ('this is six years old so it's difficult to find spare parts y' know'), it all gets mighty stressful.

There is a strange law of merchandising which says that you can buy all your electrical goods in one store, but the repair people are scattered throughout the Greater Auckland Area, and each one is a specialist in only one appliance. Of course, it goes without saying that nothing breaks down within the guarantee period.

Take our household for instance. Usually, our household runs relatively smoothly. It has to! And, we are relatively kind to our appliances. But are they grateful? Never. In the last fortnight, and I would not have the imagination to make this up:

- our dishwasher gave out smoke signals and sparks

- our washing machine suffered from incontinence
- the fuzzy fringe that had gradually grown around our TV screen became so fulsome that it obliterated the screen
- our microwave happily rotated and the light went on but actually heating the food seemed to be beyond its capabilities
- the light that stopped us falling down our front steps died
- a previously healthy torch, that could at least have prevented injury from the above-mentioned, gave up the ghost
- our fan heater refused to fan so that the heating options became distinctly dangerous.

So you now know who is single-handedly responsible for the economic upturn in the service industry. (I don't expect sympathy about our four-foot pane of glass cracking because it is not strictly speaking an electrical appliance.)

The stress in our house has been terrific. My fingers are worn out from 'doing the walking'. I have had tradesmen calling in the middle of work, I have traipsed around half of the Greater Auckland Area to specialist places, and I fear a hernia from carrying anything that is slightly smaller than the washing machine, and therefore deemed portable.

And what about my original thesis of the Seven-Year Itch? Well, we have been married twenty-six and a half years and have survived the appliance breakdowns at the seven, fourteen and twenty-one year mark. The current crisis has come eighteen months early.

Naturally, I have devised a new theory to explain this aberration. As appliances are manufactured with the period of built-in obsolescence getting increasingly shorter, the rate of marriage breakdown is ever on the increase. It makes sense from a manu-facturer's point of view. One household, one set of appliances — two households, double the sales.

But we are starting a campaign. Vernon and I are going to fox the system. We will weather the storm, fight the odds, repair and regroup the appliances and march on together. Would anyone care to join a support group?

— *East & Bays Courier*

Kiss it better, Mummy

WE ARE LIVING IN AN ERA OF Holistic Health when scientists are working out why ancient, so-called primitive, cures and remedies work. Every now and then, we read an article telling us that they have analysed the components of some long-used herb or bark distillation and — wow! — the significant component is exactly the same as the synthetic one they have been using for the past 25 years.

Why, it is only in the recent past that they have had to acknowledge that breast milk is well designed for babies and has more vital ingredients than formula. Forgive the sarcasm, but have they been in the jungle or something for the past hundred years?

A lot of this research is funded by drug companies and I have a message for them. It's about time they found out the ingredients of the best cure of all — a mother's kiss.

Every one of us who has ever been a child knows that Mummy's kisses contain tranquillisers, painkillers, antibiotics and coagulants. A normal dose contains both instant and slow release components, contains no artificial additives, no food colourings, no salicylates, no MSG and is cholesterol free. It is also non-fattening.

Should the normal dose not work immediately, it can be taken as often as required and it is impossible to overdose. Long-term effects are a feeling of well-being and warmth and a boost in self-esteem.

This cure comes attractively packaged in easy-to-use form.

(It does seem a little tasteless to say the container is biodegradable, but it is important to keep us Greenies happy.) None of the ingredients will harm the ozone layer and there are no special disposal problems.

Though the supply is unlikely to run out, there are alternatives in an emergency. Daddies, Grandmas and Grandpas are a pretty good substitute as long as you don't try to convince recipient or original donor that they are as good as the 'real thing'.

No need to pay for expensive advertising and promotion. Everyone who needs to know, already knows where to get them and there is no regulation — yet — that says you can't get them on Sundays or Public Holidays. They are widely stocked and supplies seem to be efficiently replenished as there are always more available when they are needed. So far, they haven't been patented, only the generic brand is available, and the government hasn't passed a law against it.

Perhaps it would be wiser not to ask the drug companies or the scientists to investigate. After all, what help will it be to know the ingredients? The natural product has stood the test of time. The world's resources are not threatened. And the secret recipe is being handed down very nicely, thank you, from one generation to the next.

— East & Bays Courier

Raising good problem-solvers

THE MOST IMPORTANT GIFT that we can give our children on their journey towards eventual independence, and beyond, is the ability to solve their own problems wisely. (Why else would we bother to present our children with so many problems?) We, inadvertently, prevent this process in two important ways.

First, we think it is helpful to get involved, find out who is at fault, who is to blame.

>Your child: Emily was mean to me.
>You: Well, what did *you* do to Emily?

This instantly puts our children on the defensive, and we all know that while they are watching their back — and front! — and sides! — there is no way they can do a bit of thoughtful problem-solving.

There are other ways we tend to start a blaming sentence.

>'Well why didn't you . . . ?'
>'Why is it always you who . . . ?'

These are the great stoppers to solving problems, but they do enhance our children's ability to place the responsibility elsewhere. They rapidly learn to begin with 'It's not my fault'.

Second, most of us Mothers think that the best way to teach children to problem solve is to point out the error of their ways, and to offer alternatives. Our children often seem to resist our wisdom by a technique called 'Mother Deafness'. That is, of course, why we are forced to repeat ourselves at ever increasing volumes.

> You: 'Why can't you just play nicely? How about you two go and play with your dolls?'
> Your Child: 'No-o-o-o-o. She's awful. I hate her.'
> You: 'How about you two do a puzzle?'
> Your Child: 'No-o-o-o-o. That's boring.'
> You: 'How about you two ride your bikes?'
> Your Child: 'No-o-o-o-o. We don't wanna.'

Notice that your child and the previous enemy have suddenly become 'we'. Notice who is doing all the work. Notice who is watching you do all the work. Notice your child does not like any of your ideas. Notice who is the most relaxed. Notice who is quite sure, based on previous experience, that you will keep on working to find a solution to their problem.

The other extreme is to disengage completely. 'Just ignore her', 'You sort it out', and 'Stop whining', are all good ways of convincing your children that the problem is too hard for anyone to solve and that nobody is there for them.

So what is a Mother, caught unwittingly with a child's problem, to do?

Put your arm around your child. Say, with enormous sympathy, 'That's awful for you' and wait patiently. Our job is not to problem-solve, our job is not to help our child tough it out.

Our job is to enable our children to solve age-appropriate problems. And provided we give our children emotional support, in other words, brief empathy, a listening ear and a cuddle for as long as they need, our children will run off and go back to playing with Emily *or* decide to do something else.

Either way, our children have solved their own age-appropriate problem and know they have our support. And *we* don't have to rack our brains for a solution.

— *East & Bays Courier*

Limited choice

A KINDERGARTEN TEACHER RANG me one day to ask for some advice. As a by-line to her conversation, she said, 'We have been using the Diane Levy Limited Choice Method with a great deal of success'. At this point, although I had no idea that I had developed such a method, I was immensely happy to take responsibility for anything that was successful, and began to rack my brains.

My recollection of all Limited Choice methods was 'Give your child two choices, either of which suits you fine'. And that was supposed to work in two ways. First, your child would feel consulted and therefore would be more likely to be co-operative. Second, your child would be learning to make choices — a useful skill to develop.

Example: 'Would you like to wear your green sweatshirt or your red sweatshirt?' Child chooses one or other. Child is happy, mother is happy. Method is deemed a success. This is an excellent theory and can be propounded by anyone who has not dealt with real children.

Now let's try the real world that mothers live in. Notice how much more creative real children are. 'Would you like to wear your green sweatshirt or your red one?' At this point, there is one unlikely response — see above — and several likely responses. I intend to list a small sample, of the latter, gleaned in a familiar place called Home.

> 'I want to wear the yellow one.'
> 'I'm going to wear a t-shirt.'

'I don't want to get dressed.'
'I'm hungry.'
'After I've finished this programme.'

Resist all temptation to argue, cajole, wheedle, remonstrate, think again or chase your child around the room, house, section or district. It's time to use the now remembered Diane Levy Limited Choice Method. Stand your ground, draw yourself up to your full height and proclaim with confidence 'That's not an option'.

Now comes the trickiest bit. Don't say anything else.

In order to help you maintain silence at this point, mutter repeatedly the mantra K.I.S.S. until the urge to speak has vanished. This could take some time.

KISS is a mnemonic for Keep it Simple, Stupid, and has been revived for the business world to help people write clear memos. At the coalface, called Home, one ponders upon whom 'Stupid' might refer to. Personally, I find the term 'Stupid' insulting. However, it is so offensive that it brings me up short and makes me think of the many ways I may be Stupid.

- I am Stupid if I believe that the Limited Choice Method, whoever originated it, could be executed without child protest and mayhem.
- I am Stupid if I have just racked my brains to come up with a simple two-item choice, declared it and then, at the instigation of a short person, get myself hooked into thinking up other ideas.
- I am Stupid if I believe that my child needs explanations or repetitions, as an alternative to making the choice.

To summarise. Give the choice. Respond 'That's not an option' to all unreasonable alternatives. Mutter K.I.S.S. as long as necessary. Await results. They may surprise you.

— *East & Bays Courier*

Baby talk and phone talk

THREE APPARENTLY UNCONNECTED THOUGHTS have been whirling around in my brain. Since, as my twenty-two-year-old son scornfully reminds me whenever I present him with a new brainwave of mine, 'There is no such thing as an original idea, merely the recombining of someone else's ideas', it may be time to reflect.

Thought One: I was reading a business management book yesterday which stated, 'Don't be a process consultant without having some content knowledge as well'. While I don't rate too highly my knowledge of business management, I do value my experience as a counsellor, and distinguishing between process and content is often important.

Thought Two: I have been asked to speak about adolescence and am searching for a way to convince my audience that this is not an extraordinary time of life, but rather a repetition of having a two-year-old, now extremely tall and with the addition of a massive dose of hormones. One of the issues I will want to address is 'Do adolescents really *need* to spend all that time on the phone? Is there any purpose to this behaviour?'

Thought Three: I have been looking at a video of our younger daughter when she was a baby, and have been pondering the psychological developmental purpose of her mother saying, 'Whose cute little toes-y woes-ys are these?' followed by the mother and daughter shrieking with delight.

It is all really about process rather than content. Clearly, the baby has often found all her toes attached to the same body. She has audited or stock-taken (depending on whether you want the accounting or retail system of toe addition — see how business jargon creeps in everywhere!) most mornings and discovered the same number of toes as yesterday. And yet, and we do have video evidence, she is delighted with her mother's amazingly cogent question, particularly if Mum follows it up with an exposition about 'Piggies going to Market'.

Furthermore, you would think her mother should have been able to predict confidently the ownership of the aforesaid digits since she had confirmed this, with equal delight for them both, after her daughter's bath the previous night.

So, the shared enjoyment and excitement between parent and child over ten perfectly ordinary and predictable appendages, would have to be about process rather than content.

Similarly, now that my older daughter is past the phase, I rather regret wasting my breath on the number of times I said to her during adolescence, 'What on earth could you possibly have to say to each other that hasn't already been said twenty times today? After all, you've just spent the whole day at school together *and* travelled home on the bus. You must have said it all'.

So kids, if you are reading this. The next time your parents deliver the above speech while you're on the phone, just excuse yourself to your friend, put your hand over the mouthpiece (of the phone, not the parent, that is) and say gently, kindly, yet firmly, 'You see Mum and Dad, it's a matter of process not content'.

— *East & Bays Courier*

Reflecting the real world

IT IS A PARENT'S JOB to reflect the Real World. Within the safety of home, with the support of their parents, our children will find out how the Real World operates, how it impinges on them. Well that's the theory anyway.

I believe this theory fervently, but it never ceases to amaze me how often the Real World conspires against parents. Take school lunches, for instance. Well that, literally, is what we would like our children to do. We would like them to remember to *take* their lunches to school!

I believe that it is important that we do not continue to be our children's 'reminders' — as in 'Put your lunchbox in your bag,' 'Have you remembered your track shoes?', 'You must take your raincoat — I don't care if it sucks. That's probably a good characteristic in a raincoat'.

Sometimes the Real World conspires against mothers. Last time my daughter forgot her lunch I fretted all morning, recalling dire warnings about pupils who cannot concentrate because of inadequate nutrition, and practised sitting on my hands so that I couldn't dial the school number to make suggestions or drive to school to rescue the situation.

'How was school today?' I asked with feigned casualness. I wanted to write 'feigned casualty', but that's what the house is like between

7.15 and 7.45 a.m. on a weekday!

'Wonderful', she declared. 'When I found I had no lunch, I cried. So the teacher sent me to the office, and they lent me money, and so I went up the road to the dairy with one of the big girls. I bought potato chips and a fizzy drink in a can. You have to give the school four dollars and I can't wait to forget my lunch again.'

I have long suspected the fickleness of the Real World, but does it really have to take a swipe at mothers who give children wholemeal sandwiches and fresh fruit?

Another time, I decided that I had written enough children's school speeches, and so this third child could learn the skills from the Real World. She had rejected all offers of help anyway, so I had to think up a Theory of Child Rearing to cover my Pain of Rejection.

She did practise the final product on us before presentation. It was a terrifying speech. No sensible caring parent could possibly have written this one. (At least I didn't have to modify it to make it look like a seven-year-old had written it). The speech began along the lines of 'When I am principal of the school we will all go to McDonald's for morning tea. Then we'll do Art until lunchtime'. Further details of a profligate life followed.

Once again, Real World mother asked cautiously, 'How was your school day?' Apparently the speech had been received like a Billy Graham rally. Every sentence received an ovation, and she finally resumed her seat to thunderous applause.

I have a certain, smug satisfaction in knowing that she won't be able to carry off the same effect with her speech on Captain Cook.

— East & Bays Courier

Let's not tell the first fib

NONE OF US SET out to teach our children to lie, but it is little short of amazing what a good job we do.

At first, our children believe we know everything, hear everything and can see through walls, several, if necessary. There's nothing like a bit of silence to alert us to danger signals. 'It's too quiet in there' we think, and we are usually right.

Occasionally, we misjudge, roar into the room, only to find our children absorbed in some harmless pastime. After a couple of errors in this direction, we learn the 'Parental Saunter'.

The 'Parental Saunter' goes like this. You hear an ominous silence from the other end of the house. Scarred by the last time you misjudged, you race quietly down the corridor, screech silently to a halt about ten feet from target, and then saunter into the room as if you just remembered you had to get something important out of the cupboard.

Big, innocent eyes gaze at you. 'How nicely you are playing' or, depending on the activity, 'You know full well that is not allowed', you declaim, leaving your child wondering 'How did she know?' Our aim is that our children will eventually internalise 'Dragon Mother Knows Everything' into a fully-fledged Conscience. This process takes at least eight years.

So where does it all come unstuck? How do we teach our children to tell such amazingly convincing, so convincing they have convinced themselves, stories. It usually starts with the Cookie Jar.

'What's that brown stuff round your mouth?' we ask accusingly.

'Nothing,' they say, hopeful that this will get them off the hook.

'Come and look in the mirror. I'll show you nothing,' we say, marching them to the nearest mirror.

'It must be paint', the miscreant suggests, doing their best to please.

'Taste it,' we command, trusting the Health Inspector wasn't peeking in as we licked our finger, scraped off the offending substance and stuck our chocolatey finger in the child's mouth.

'O-o-o-h! It tastes like chocolate,' says the utterly surprised thief.

'How did it get there?' we demand.

'A witch must have flown in the window and painted it on.'

By now, we are so hooked into believing that we have raised a congenital liar, with no regard for the truth or morality, that we are only a tiny step away from — or have already arrived at — hysteria.

In fact, *we* uttered the first lie. What! Honest me a liar? Well, who was it who said 'What's that around your mouth?' when we already knew the answer? Our child knew that we knew and that we found it unacceptable. So they were just trying to improve on the original to please us, or stay out of trouble, or both.

So what is a parent supposed to do? Don't be the first one to lie, don't help the lie carry on. Use all your vigilance, wit, wisdom, instinct and low cunning to stay fully and secretly informed. If you are not sure, stay alert, gather more evidence.

If your child has done something wrong, state the crime and state the consequence. Help your child to accept responsibility for their actions by 'repairing damages' where possible.

Practise all you can in the 'Cookie-Jar Era'. You will need the same skills during 'The Big A' — adolescence. And your vigilance will have to be higher, and your cunning will have to be a lot lower!

— *East & Bays Courier*

I wish I knew *the* parenting trick . . .

MANY OF US SEARCH PARENTING LITERATURE in the hope that we will find a trick to help us through the latest test our child is throwing at us. I use the word 'trick' advisedly.

Collins Concise Dictionary defines 'trick' as:

1. a deceitful or cunning trick or plan;
2. a humorous or mischievous action or plan;
3. an illusory or magic feat;
4. a simple feat learned by an animal or person;
5. an adroit or ingenious device; knack;
   and most pertinent of all, in my opinion,
6. *do the trick* — to produce the desired result.

In other words, when our children throw the latest curly our way — whether it is hurling themselves on the ground like an animated starfish, using the bedroom carpet as their very own en suite loo, attaching their duvet to the bottom sheet with bubble gum so the bed is easier to make, or storing fifteen used coffee cups in their bedroom (each one cradling an apple core) — we want a swift, efficient and painless way to handle the situation. In other words, a trick.

What is more, we want a trick that will work forever *or* avert that particular behaviour for a very long time *or* can be used easily and repeatedly. In other words, we want child rearing to be rather like painting a bookcase. We may be prepared to do the work, but we expect the effect to last for many years.

Sorry folks. I wish it could be like that, but I fear that child rearing is far more akin to maintaining a lawn. No matter how well you mow the grass, there it is, all ready to be done again a fortnight later.

Sure, sometimes we get lucky and the effect lasts for three weeks. But this is more than under-compensated for by the times it needs doing in a week's time. And there is no doubt that raising a child involves a lot of trimming around the edges.

And where does the weeding come in to all this — not to mention mulching, pruning and fertilising? It doesn't really bear thinking about. The truth is I have no idea, but I do know that, just as our real lawn is subject to weed seeds sprouting up, dogs and cats doing unmentionable things and kids making bike tracks and lighting fires, our 'parenting lawn' is also subject to many influences from outside our family and often beyond our control.

To follow our analogy one step further, regardless of where the extraneous influence comes from, we are the only ones who are responsible for dealing with the consequence and putting our little seedlings back on track.

I was once told that the recipe for a beautiful bowling green is to plant the finest seed, water it and roll it for twenty years.

There are no parenting short cuts. But it will never stop me searching for an easier way.

— East & Bays Courier

It's concert time again

A FEW WEEKS AGO I heard John Cooney, of *Grapevine* fame, speaking. He talked about the time when his children were in their very early teens and he bought a small yacht — so small that he used to wheel it around in a wheelbarrow.

Together, he and his children painted the yacht, maintained it, learned to sail it, and sailed it. A few years later, it lay untouched. The children had lost interest and gone on to further peer group activities of mid-adolescence.

The point John made was that, as parents, we have these short bursts of activity with our children and then that particular interactive phase is past. The important message is to enjoy and value that phase, because you never get that particular opportunity again.

And so I was determined to get every amount of enjoyment out of my daughter's Jazz Ballet Concert season. It's a great process that takes over our lives for a fortnight. I use the word 'our' advisedly, since the extended family becomes involved in finding a magnificent jewel to hold the feather on the turban, complex transport arrangements, rehearsals at inconvenient times and attending Our Star's performances.

Mothers gather in little clusters at the first costume rehearsal and speak in a whole new in-crowd language. 'Did you glue or stick the sequins?' 'How do you stop gold lamé from laddering?' 'I wasn't issued with a feather.' 'The best way to do stage make-up is to think of K Road and double it.' 'Are you going to curl, frizz or rag her hair?'

Grandparents for whom 'rap' is something you spell differently and do to parcels, sit through booming music, inhale clouds of dry ice and search diligently amongst twenty little Stars for theirs. If they are lucky that will receive strict instructions like 'I'm second from the right in the first row after the Sailor Dance and eleventh in the Finale'.

We all become a magnificent sisterhood. We sit backstage for hours armed with safety pins, potato chips, paracetamol and spare lipsticks. Every child is checked with loving care before their Grand Entrance.

I watch from the wings hardly able to see because sentimental tears are flowing. The children are so keen, so excited and such great performers. I feel so proud of all of them — and so proud of mine. We usher them back to the dressing room to await the Grand Finale.

Off they go again. Back onto the stage to take their bows. Families re-group in the cool night air. We take our little troupers home. We wash off inches of make-up. We tuck the by-now-exhausted-and-grouchy Star into bed.

We repeat this process four times in three days. We put the costume away, re-allocate the make-up. If we are lucky there may be a fancy-dress party next April so we can use the masterpiece costume again. A few days later, we find the programme and the used tickets scrunched under her bed. *We* put it in her scrapbook.

When we complain pridefully about all the associated hardships to our friends with older children, they become misty-eyed. They remember it as a special phase that is gone.

— *East & Bays Courier*

It must be Christmas

IF I WERE A recently arrived Martian, I would know it was Christmas time.

At the end of November, the 'junk mail' contributions to my letterbox advertise all manner of Christmas decorations I could buy. I would easily be able to understand that A Tree was required and that upon this tree I should be placing all sorts of glorious baubles designed to be lit or to catch the light. What is more, I would easily be able to grasp the idea that several different companies were trying to persuade me to buy their tree and their decorations.

By the end of the first week of December, judging by the letterbox drop, I would understand that lots and lots of presents for family members were mandatory. It would be very clear to me that they must be bought, that the price was very important and that specific wrapping was needed.

By the middle of December, trusting my learning to the same University of the Letterbox, I would comprehend the need to stock up on expensive meats such as ham and turkey and to buy some cranberry sauce. Now cranberry sauce is a bit of a mystery to the newly immigrated Martian mind, because I have never seen a cranberry grow near Auckland. I haven't seen cherries or mistletoe either, come to think of it. So I wonder what it is all about.

If I listened to my radio, I could hear all sorts of advertisements explaining to me that I should not worry if I could not afford all of this now. There seems to be a lot of people assuming that, even if I do not have the money now, I will miraculously have it in February because I can, so I am told, pay it back then.

There were other things that puzzled my Martian mind. I looked at Christmas cards and saw a beautiful star and snow and plum puddings and holly. I had never seen those in Auckland before.

Martians are pretty thoughtful creatures, so I wondered why I should be doing all this. At first, judging by what came through the letterbox, I thought it might be a festival for sacrificing trees.

So I checked with my earthling friends. They explained to me that we were doing all this because their parents and their grandparents had done this, and they remembered it with enormous fondness. They liked to do the same thing because it helped them bring back all the warm fuzzy feelings.

They also liked to get together with family, because that helped them stay connected. Sometimes there were family rows on the day, but it was nearly always worth it. There was usually lots of work for the host lady, but it all felt worth it when she saw everyone happy. (A male earthling told me that one!)

Of course, some people felt very lonely and left out when they thought everyone else was with family except them. And some people sacrificed more money than they could manage, because they wanted their children to have a good time. And some children, who belong to two parents in separate households, got shredded. And some people celebrated a little too hard and a little too much.

'Where did it all start?' I asked my earthling friend. So I heard a beautiful story from a long time ago. The story was about love and peace, goodwill and tradition, sharing and spirituality, caring for and valuing each other.

So I went back to my letterbox and wondered why it had forgotten to tell me about the real meaning of Christmas.

— East & Bays Courier

Sorry kids! I've got all the time in the world

DEAR KIDS,

I don't want to upset you and I do want you to have a good holiday. But I have to inform you that I too am on holiday and I've got all the time in the world.

This means that the old tricks simply won't work. One of the best tricks you have perfected is 'running out of time'. During term time we all have commitments and have to get out the door. If you cannot dress yourself in time, I do it for you because sending you to your place of learning in your pyjamas reflects badly upon mothers.

All year I would have loved to be able to say, 'Until you are dressed and ready, we are not going anywhere'. It simply was not practical to do that, what with the car-pool, your mat time and my meeting time. But now, I really don't care if you choose to spend all morning in your room.

All year I've coaxed you to eat breakfast so you wouldn't be a deprived child who couldn't concentrate on her schoolwork because her mother didn't care enough to give her a nutritious breakfast. Now that I can sin in private there won't be breakfast until you are dressed and your bed is made. If it takes all morning, don't worry. You can find me sitting with my feet up, drinking coffee and reading today's paper.

I feel guilty about the way I have neglected you in term time. There simply has not been time to instruct you, and then let you learn through practice, essential skills that you may need. Now that I am on holiday I would be happy to help you learn. By the end of the holidays you will be impressed at your competence at peeling vegetables, hand washing small and large items, managing without a dishwasher, setting and clearing tables and preparing simple meals.

You may not, of course, share my joy at your new learnings. You may find it necessary to fuss, cry, shout, moan and grizzle. That's OK with me. During term time, I want you to go to school happy and ready to face the day and learn a lot. I want me to arrive at work looking calm, radiating energy and confidence. So I'll do almost anything to avoid noisy confrontation. During the holidays, I can cope with your being upset in private. You can have a great day or a miserable one. I'm going to have a great day. When you are ready to join me, you'll know where to find me.

Holidays are great times to play. You play children's games and I'll play adult games. I don't play with children to entertain them (the best playmate for a seven-year-old is a contemporary, or better still, several contemporaries) but sometimes I love to play at children's games with pleasant children and be a child myself.

Provided it's voluntary, and not coerced by whining, I'm great at losing swing-ball, losing the Frisbee, doing handstands underwater, being the noisiest at Animal Snap, burying most of you in sand and picking up crabs at low tide. Just remember that all these things are only fun when they are not compulsory. That is why it is called Play.

And about being bored. Don't bother. You have a house full of toys and the most beautiful country in the world to live in and enjoy. All term time we rush around — exhausted, excited, over-committed, stressed, tense and watching the clock.

Come and tell me if you are bored. 'That's wonderful,' I'll say. 'I'm trying hard to be — and I might even get there in a few days!' My wristwatch is in the drawer.

— East & Bays Courier

Sandcastles

I REMEMBER THE SUMMERS of my youth. Factories closed down for three weeks so the family hired a bach for exactly that amount of time. The skies were clear blue every day, all day and we all tanned ourselves black, which seemed a very good idea at the time.

It's strange how things come around again. We conserved the water because it came out of our tank — the sole source. We were far too modest, in those days, to recite doggerel about flushing down brown and mellowing yellow, but I recall treasured trumpet lilies growing profusely around the long-drop door.

For the benefit of the young pioneers of today, let me explain. Trumpet lilies were to long-drops what today's Countryair is to loos. And about as ineffective. These beautiful flowers were odourless by day, but gave off a magnificent perfume at night. I think nature let us down a bit there. We could have done with the perfume at the hottest point of the day.

What set me off, on this trip down memory lane, was witnessing my daughter's participation in a Sandcastle Competition. For starters, it was a wonderful experience to see fifty children, bottoms up, heads down, concentrating and co-operating for a solid hour. No one paused to draw breath to ask for a cold can of anything fizzy, to say 'I'm bored', or to tell me they needed new batteries. They worked like little beavers. Come to think of it they even looked like little beavers!

The best bit was THEY WEREN'T VERY GOOD AT IT! Now I bet you think I am being petty, ungracious and churlish. True. But in this age where four-year-olds know more about computers than I do and six-year-olds manage the switches, the correct distance to hold a microphone and speaking through it, with more aplomb than I will ever be able to muster, I unashamedly take revenge.

The modern generation knows very little about moats, tunnelling and how far down you need to dig to reach water. Not for them the satisfaction of building a huge mound, carefully compacted for structural strength. They haven't sampled the joys of four friends lying face down in hot sand, burrowing to your armpits ever so carefully through the sand-mountain until your hands meet in the middle.

I offered to show them the finer points. I gathered an unwilling horde, well three of them anyway, and marched them down to the beach to the Technical Institute of the Sandcastle. I dug and heaved and compacted, pausing only for the odd breath to proclaim 'Isn't this great fun?' I put their non-response down to their being overwhelmed at my skill.

I had just got to the centre of my tunnel, full arm-length, awaiting the feel of a trusting little hand or three reaching out for mine, when I heard a voice say, 'You OK lady?'

From my would-be rescuer's point of view, the scene looked like this. A deserted beach. A large middle-aged lady face down in the sand with her arm pinned by a huge sandcastle. And the tide coming in.

Isn't it nice to know that the modern generation cares?

— *East & Bays Courier*

Did I really need to shout so loud?

PICTURE THE SCENE. I had been flattened by some dreadful 'lurg' that caused me to spend eight hours of darkness perched upon the loo with my arm wrapped around a large bowl. I occupied myself during this long night by alternately moaning pathetically and using both receptacles simultaneously with considerable force and no aplomb whatsoever.

Naturally, when dawn broke, and throughout the following thirty six hours, I was not at my parenting best. To add insult to injury, we were going away for a fortnight's holiday.

To my considerable relief, our nine-year-old offered to make lunch for the family prior to our departure. After much 'to-ing and fro-ing' and folding of serviettes into artistic shapes, we were summoned to the table.

Since I am about to describe some pretty disgraceful behaviour on my part (presuming myself to be a mature, grown adult who has been heard to profess she loves her children) I will try to claim your sympathy by listing my expectations and excuses.

First, I was feeling exceedingly frail. Second, we were about to go away. Third, I needed the fridge to be left relatively empty and assumed that my daughter knew this.

I therefore came to the table anticipating all manner of leftovers and half-empty containers to be arranged thereon, and expected the family to co-operate in their consumption. ('Waste not, want not' comes into that somewhere.)

I arrived to find the sole edible items on the table were a newly thawed loaf of sliced bread, and a concoction consisting of two cans of tuna, chopped tomatoes and mayonnaise. I did what any self-respecting two-year-old does when confronted with disappointment and frustration. I had a colossal and extremely noisy tantrum. It must have been impressive because everyone's mouth gaped in utter astonishment and they became totally and tensely silent. Not surprisingly, the chef retired in a flood of tears.

About two hours later, as we drove away on our happy holiday in miserable silence, I did contemplate apologising. The problem was that the apology list was too long and by now I was too remorseful to action it. I longed to be two years old, mutter 'Sorry', however insincerely, and be forgiven and allowed to watch Playschool.

There was one saving grace. I reminded myself that there are better ways of teaching a child than screaming at them what they did wrong. The next time Deborah offered to help — and it is a tribute to the forgiving nature and the resilience of children that she even contemplated helping again — I remembered that the time to set parameters is *before* the event.

I discussed with her what was suitable, hung around to coach her through the tricky bits and joined the family in appreciation of her achievement. That felt like good parenting. It would be nice to be perfect all the time, wouldn't it? But then we wouldn't be real parents.

— *East & Bays Courier*

The new school year

LEADING UP TO THE start of the new school year, articles of advice abound for parents whose children are starting school. You would think that five-year-olds were the only people who started school and parents of five-year-olds were the only ones with problems. Frankly, I feel a little left out.

Every school year brings with it its own starting problems. Where was the paragraph dealing with 'How to get the mould out of the school cushion that has spent six hot, humid weeks under your child's bed and it is now midnight'? Who cared about 'finding old HB pencils longer than two centimetres'? Where were the comforting suggestions on what to say to your twelve-year-old who visits you at 2.00 a.m. to say, 'What if I am not in the same class as Maryanne?' How come drink-bottle lids evaporate on 31 January?

The 'biggie' that I believe is never addressed is 'How much homework will I (the parent) be responsible for this year?' I know the theory. We are responsible for support, encouragement and supervision, but Homework is essentially a contract between teacher and pupil. Homework is about allowing children to experience the consequences of their actions or, more aggravatingly, their inactions.

It's a great theory, but it completely ignores the fact that some years are more important than others. Year One, Year Two and Year Three are so important with regard to making sure you have a competent and happy reader, that full home support for the process is essential.

Year Four brings the broadening of writing and research skills — well, the parent's ability to research actually — so our support is needed. I hope you noticed that use of the word 'support'. If you are a real parent you will know that this is psychobabble for 'nag, scream, shout and tear your hair out'. This also seems to be the year for first time projects, speeches, times tables and newspapers. So, again the afore described support is required.

Then there are the 'first' years, Years Seven and Nine, when it is essential that your child has a good start and makes a good impression. Guess Who makes it Her business to see that it happens. And, of course, the exam years, Years Eleven, Twelve and Thirteen, need a Mum.

What I am about to reveal is usually said only in private between consenting adults, so I am going to take the risk and reveal all. Some years you need a good school report to gain entry to the next school. These years also require your unrelenting input. They are — Year Six and Year Eight.

This leaves only two years in your child's entire school career, where you can honour the theoretical Homework contract and leave it to the Pupil-Teacher relationship to sort out. There is Year Ten. I have grave reservations about this one. I am so grateful to anyone who will assume some care for my child at this stroppy stage, that the school not only has my full support, but also my undying gratitude.

So that leaves only Year Five, and this year our youngest started this joyous year. I was going to have a year off, my last till she left school, if I believe what I write. I was going to let her take full responsibility for her homework.

She came home from school on her first day. Afternoon tea at the ready, I sat at the kitchen table for chat and 'hang around while she does her homework at the kitchen table' time. 'Thanks Mum. I'll just take the food to my desk and do my homework,' she said and vanished behind a closed door.

I lasted five minutes!

'Need any help?'
'No thanks, Mum.'
'Can I see your homework?'
'Sure.'
I had forgotten how interesting their homework is these days. What is a 'murder of crows,' anyway?
'Can I look it up for you?'
'No thanks, Mum.'
I consulted three dictionaries and a thesaurus.
'I think I have the answer.'
'No worries, Mum, I've finished it all now.'

Non-interference is going to be trickier than I thought. I just might have to go back to being supportive.

— East & Bays Courier

Building a cathedral

I WAS READING AN article in December's *Fortune* magazine entitled 'Why do we work?' It began with the following story:

'In the days of misty towers, distressed maidens, and stalwart knights, a young man, walking along the road, came upon a labourer fiercely pounding away at a stone with a hammer and chisel. The lad asked the worker, who looked frustrated and angry, 'What are you doing?' The labourer answered in a pained voice, 'I am trying to shape this stone and it is backbreaking work.'

The youth continued his journey and soon came upon another man chipping away at a similar stone, who looked neither particularly angry nor happy. 'What are you doing?' he asked. 'I'm shaping a stone for a building.'

The young man went on and before long came to a third worker chipping away at a stone, but this worker was singing happily as he worked. 'What are you doing?' The worker smiled and replied, 'I am building a cathedral.'

The article's byline to 'Why do we work?' is 'Sure, it's for money. But more and more people, realising that's not all there is to life, are embarking on a new search for meaning in corporate America.'

Well, I have news for the author, Brian Dumaine. We, the mothers of New Zealand and, I suspect, those mothers who spawned 'corporate America', have known for a long time that no one could pay us enough money for the work we do. Further, the reason that we work so hard and so willingly, is because every day we are 'building cathedrals'.

Raising a child to independent adulthood is cathedral-building work. Just like the labourer chipping away looking frustrated and angry, a lot of our work can be thought of as tedious, repetitive, unappreciated and backbreaking.

You will notice that I did not include the word 'soul-destroying'. That is because, like the third labourer, we choose not to itemise our Job Description into categories like nose-wiping, nappy changing, shouting orders, night-watchman, spell-checker, door monitor, puddle-soaker-*extraordinaire*. We see the overview. We are working towards the completion of our cathedrals.

When next you visit a cathedral give some thought, not only to the architect and the project manager, but also to the many artisans without whom the project could not have been completed.

When next you see a child, an adolescent, an adult, or any half-way decent human being, remember the architect, the project manager and the artisans, all of whom are wrapped into one person who answers to the call of 'Mu-u-u-m'.

And when next you see me cuddling my child, don't be surprised if I say 'Sh-h-h-h! I'm building a cathedral!'

— *East & Bays Courier*

Showing off is so very hard to do

IT WAS A WONDERFUL coincidence. Deborah, our nine-year-old, and I had leisure time at the same time. 'Choose any place you would like to have afternoon tea in Mission Bay,' I said, imagining I was offering a large range of options. The Golden Arches Café, of course. Silly question.

'M-u-u-um,' she began tentatively. Since *tentative* is not her usual life-position, I was on full alert. 'Do you think you could write something nice about me for once in your articles?' In my own defence, I have to state that this was from a child who asks, wistfully, every time I write, 'Will you be writing about me?'

Of course a wave of guilt dumped all over me. I wondered how much damage I had done to a frail little emergent ego. (I entirely forgot that the ego had emerged rampant by about two months and has continued to rampage ever since.) I wondered if I should give up writing. I wondered if I should give up counselling. I wondered if I was fit to parent anyone. Never let it be said that mothers aren't good at catastrophic thoughts.

The question has been haunting me every day. Not because of 'the guilt bit', but because I keep thinking how hard it is for us to publicly declare that we adore our children, that *ours* are absolutely the most splendid human beings in the whole world.

I heartily subscribe to the maxim that 'Every child deserves to have at least one parent who is irrationally crazy about them.' But I squirm at the thought of describing, out loud, the wonderful characteristics of my children.

Not speaking up flies directly in the face of enhancing our children's self-esteem so that they will grow up resilient and able to take the inevitable knocks that life dishes out. It mocks the idea that if a child likes themself, they will be able to say 'No' and resist peer pressure when appropriate.

It is partly upbringing about not showing off. It is partly superstition about saying something nice causes it to disappear. It is partly Kiwi understatement. It is partly Tall Poppy stuff. These are my excuses.

We are so comfortable speaking about all the things that drive us up the wall. We so easily share the dreadful things our children do and say. We do not hesitate to seek support from our peers when our children are irritating, annoying and obnoxious.

OK! OK! We do share achievements with our friends. We do, with exaggerated modesty, admit to the odd certificate, medal, scholarship or smileyface sticker, particularly if someone else has heard about it first. And how often do we add a disclaimer, 'Of course, it's only because he's the oldest in the group.'

So after much hesitation and deliberation, I am coming out of the parental closet. It is true that I worry what my family, my peers and my colleagues will think. I wonder if people will stop talking to me or cross the street to avoid me. I may even get hate mail. My adult children may never speak to me again. However, now is the time for risk and declaration.

I am the mother of three wonderful children. My son is hard-working, extremely focussed, a greatly talented athlete, good-looking and has an amazingly fast and funny wit. My older daughter is beautiful, intelligent, articulate (you have no idea how difficult this is to do), a wonderful friend, incredibly independent and has great charm. My younger daughter is wonderfully strong-willed, bright as a button, very caring, a great joy to us all and a magnificent asset to our family.

There! I said it! To my amazement, my computer has not pushed its own Delete button, nor is it sending out smoke signals. It has even accepted the Print instruction.

But I am feeling so uncomfortable. I wonder what will happen next.

— East & Bays Courier

Reading rooms

I HAVE ALWAYS BELIEVED that love of books is something that is 'caught not taught'. In our home, we have a strong emphasis on reading. Forages, and I use the term advisedly, to the library demonstrate a compulsive side to our natures and the family rule, for both adults and children, has always been 'you can only take out as many books as you can carry'.

With this emphasis on literature, it will not surprise you to know that we have a Reading Room — two, in fact — one for Adults Only and one for General and Children's Reading. Anyone entering these rooms will be able to instantly tell what family members are reading because the books will be there, open, waiting for the reader to return.

You may be interested in the other furniture in our Reading Rooms. There is a comfortable white, porcelain seat complete with water and lid, a roll of paper, in a special holder, for bookmarks and a hand basin for washing off any newsprint, should that be needed. The lock on the door ensures that you cannot be interrupted in the middle of essential research. Our Reading Rooms can double up, if strictly necessary, for the maintenance of essential bodily functions.

I love to visit a particular friend's house, because her Guest and Family Reading Room doubles as a Meditation Room. Upon the walls are taped profound meditations and I always look forward to my visits there for the new learnings that await me. Last Friday, after several cups of coffee with my friend, it was clearly time for Meditation before tackling the drive home.

Wonder of wonders, there was a new/old Meditation awaiting me. Old, because I had heard it many times before. New, because I had never before thought of it as both a perfect description of, and blueprint for, excellent parenting. (I intend to elaborate upon this learning in my next article.)

I drove home trying to retain the wording in my mind. By the time early evening arrived, the essence remained but the detail had vanished.

I rang the household. My friend was out, but her husband was home. 'Could you do me a favour, please?' I asked. This lovely man was nice enough to take a portable phone, stand in his Meditation Room and carefully dictate, phrase by phrase, complete with punctuation, patiently waiting for me to write slowly in long-hand, the following Irish Blessing. That is true generosity of spirit.

> 'May the road rise to meet you,
> May the wind be always at your back.
> May the sun shine warm upon your face,
> The rain fall soft upon your fields.
> And, until we meet again,
> May God hold you in the palm of his hand.'

— East & Bays Courier

Different paths

IN MY LAST ARTICLE, I quoted the following Irish Blessing and promised to return to it. The attraction, for me, was that this blessing seems to epitomise what it is we are seeking to do as parents.

> 'May the road rise to meet you,
> May the wind be always at your back.
> May the sun shine warm upon your face,
> The rain fall soft upon your fields.
> And, until we meet again,
> May God hold you in the palm of his hand.'

This is what we parents so often try to do for our children. We want the path to 'rise to meet' them. We want to help them choose a path that we believe suits their needs, their wants and their ambitions and their temperament.

Of course, we sometimes confuse *our* needs with *their* needs. Usually when we attempt to do this, our child will remind us with a 'Yeah, Mum, yeah! That's what *you'd* do but its not what *I'd* do.' We would do well to heed this message, however painful. Our children are usually accurate on this one. It is also a signal that they are determined to do it *their* way and are most unwilling to be persuaded otherwise.

We try hard to swing them in a direction so that the 'wind will be at their back and the sun will shine warm upon their face'. Yet how often do our children seem determined to take the path where the wind is likely to blow them off their feet. They sometimes seem absolutely resolute that the only path that will do is the one where the sun rarely shines or glares dangerously and damagingly.

The vision I wish for when I read 'the rain fall soft upon your fields' is that life will deal gently and kindly with my children. It also embodies, for me, the concept of all the gentle nurturing we do as parents. In spite of all this, or possibly, because of this tender building up of their resilience, there will be times when our children seek the thunder, the lightning, the stormiest way.

We may talk rationally and sensibly about the dangers of this path or the wisdom of taking that path. We may yell and scream the same message. We may even pretend indifference. Sometimes, our children simply have to find out for themselves, make their own discoveries.

Sometimes it seems we have no alternative but to watch our children go down a path to danger or a path to nowhere. It is at these times that we can do little but hope that 'God will hold them in the palm of his hand' while they go on a perilous journey.

And often we are forced to admit that it was from the difficult journeys that our children learned the most.

— *East & Bays Courier*

The joys of mastery

WHEN I WAS STUDYING Psychology at Auckland University, the culmination of my advanced studies was to teach a rat to tell the difference between horizontal and vertical lines. At first, I rewarded the rat *every* time it jumped to a platform which had a picture of horizontal lines above it. Once the rat had this mastered, I gave it food every second time and eventually, the rat would 'remember' the horizontal lines as long as I rewarded it occasionally.

In case this sounds like an archaic practice, it was. It was part of Behavioural Psychology in 1968. The whole purpose was to teach us that learning takes place through reinforcement. If we extrapolate that to human behaviour, we are tempted to believe that people behave a certain way solely because that behaviour is reinforced or rewarded from an external source. I believe that this is a very incomplete view.

Remember the first time your child rolled over, or took her first halting steps, or blew out his birthday candle, or managed to climb up the steps and slide down the slide? Remember clapping and dancing and exclaiming and enthusing? And remember feeling so proud — as if you personally had mastered a great feat?

I have no argument with our behaviour on these momentous occasions. I did it with my children and intend to be every bit as enthusiastic with grandchildren.

The thing that worries me is that we take this behaviour of ours

— the encouragement, reinforcement praise and enthusiasm — and imagine it actually contributed to our children's learning. It is as if we somehow have convinced ourselves that, unless we had provided all this incentive and cheerleading, our child may never have learned to roll over or to walk or to go up and down a slide.

And we extrapolate this experience into believing that our children require an endless stream of positive attention, stickers, stars on the chart and eventually pocket money, late night passes and driving lessons and 'if you get a decent pass I'll buy you a car' (which after all is only a giant star on the star chart) in order to learn essential skills.

Somewhere along the way, we have forgotten that most of us work hard and repeat tasks endlessly in order to achieve mastery. And that the joy of mastery is the reward in itself. Why else would anyone struggle to do a crossword?

Watch a toddler doing what they do best — toddling. I love the way they enjoy their own mastery, their own amazing cleverness at putting one foot in front of the other. Listen as they chuckle with delight as they practise and practise and practise for the pure joy of toddling.

Watch a preschooler learning to pour, carefully applying paint to paper, hammering nails or threading beads, and you can see the intensity of their desire to master the skill.

It certainly does not stop there. With the first chill in the air I think of the ski slopes. People of all ages doing run after run after run, purely for the joy of doing better next time. Ponder why people get satisfaction from jigsaws, bridge, tapestry, paintings or computer games.

Watch the behaviour of young men in video parlours or while you wait for your fish and chips. Watch the intensity of the youths who have mastery over a set of rapidly changing events and variables, and can maintain incredible concentration, while we cannot even work out what the game is about. If only we could help them hook this Joy of Mastery into useful and worthwhile tasks.

Consider how important it is to provide our children with the opportunity to learn a sport, a musical instrument, to read, to calculate, to spell or to ride a bike. Notice how many of these things our children approach with natural enthusiasm until we decide to be even more enthusiastic than they are.

And notice that, if we think it is our job to keep them enthusiastic, rather than to let their natural drive towards mastery lead them, how quickly they make it our job to keep them on task.

I am not suggesting that we shouldn't be present, give support and give guidance where appropriate. It's just that there is a fine line between coercing them to reach *our* goals and joining them in the pure enjoyment of *their* mastery.

So what is the message? To put it crudely, let's practise 'butting out' of our children's learning experiences. *Us* getting excited and *them* keeping us excited or disappointed, is the wrong way round.

Children need *us* to provide the opportunity and support for *them* to get excited about learning and practising and experimenting and eventually mastering the skill and moving on to the next one.

— *East & Bays Courier*

Running away

IT HAS ALWAYS FASCINATED me that children choose to run away. I'm not thinking of 'street kids' who have made a decision that living on the streets, alone or with their peers, is preferable to what there is for them at home. I'm thinking of children who appear, to our parental eyes, to have everything going for them in their home, and still think it is better elsewhere. I wonder how much of this begins in childhood.

Our two-year-old decides to 'take off'. It isn't necessary that she leave our house, just that she leave our 'orbit of control'. Maybe we have called her over to put on a sock, or to show us what she has picked up off the ground and stuffed into her mouth. It may simply be that she has done something inappropriate — the politically correct word for 'naughty' or 'wrong' or 'bad' — we believe a reprimand or consequence is in order.

Since our child appears unwilling to come to us, we indulge ourselves in a number of interesting antics. We may give chase. Since she has already decided that a large space is comfortable between her and us, the closer we get the more she has to increase the distance in order to maintain the same gap. If we run, she runs. If we stop, she stops. If we walk slowly and deliberately, she walks slowly and deliberately. What a wonderful game!

Just in case this isn't enough to entice her back, we add sound and light variations. Maybe a screaming mouth set within a bright red face will be more attractive to her, so we try that. Surprise, surprise! She runs still further.

It is time to remember that we are the parent and the centre of our child's universe. Their task is to keep safe within our orbit and to make increasingly larger forays out into the universe, knowing that they can always return safely to base when the world looks a little dangerous.

So what is a parent supposed to do? Essentially, unless your child is in danger, stay put. Sooner or later, usually sooner, your child will drift past to find out what you are doing or if you are missing her. Grab her and follow up on whatever it was you wanted in the first place.

This is great practice for when your teenagers leave dramatically declaring they cannot live with such impossible people. If you run after them, begging, flapping, cajoling, yelling or pleading, making a public spectacle or a private doormat of yourself, they will have to get away even further or stay away even longer to prove their point.

As long as they are safe, (and one of the more useful things we taught our children early was that they were free to run and stay away, as long as they went to a safe place and sent word of where they were) stay put. Be friendly and non-committal on the phone and cautiously welcoming upon their return.

Pay attention to why they left. Did they just need a bit of space *or* were there serious concerns? Ask them. They are they only ones that know.

And remember, one of the least useful things you can say is — 'If you go, you can't come back'.

— *East & Bays Courier*

Let's be civil

THE MAY/JUNE 1995 'Royal Bank Letter' published by the Royal Bank of Canada begins with an article entitled 'The Duty of Civility'. Here are a few of the points made:

- Civility means a great deal more than just being nice to one another.
- Civility is the lubricant that keeps a society running smoothly.
- It is a variation on the Golden Rule, urging that you treat everyone as decently and considerately as you would like to be treated yourself.
- Where there is civility, issues are not resolved by shouting one another down.

This sounded highly appropriate for the commercial world and the more I thought about it, the more appropriate it sounded for the world of the family. This, too, was addressed in the article. The key to civility, it stated, is in trying to make everyone you encounter day-by-day feel at ease. The spirit of civility encompasses consideration, tact, good humour and respect for others' feelings and rights.

'Great theory, Diane' I hear you say. 'I'm pretty civil at the bank. And they are pretty civil to me — as long as one of my three preschoolers doesn't need a toilet with ten seconds' warning.' Fair enough, but what about outside the bank? After all, how many of us bank at the Royal Bank of Canada?

I drifted into a fantasy of what it might be like if I treated my family with civility and they did likewise for me. Imagine if they stopped calling, from three rooms away, 'M-u-u-u-u-m' and imagine if I stopped yelling back 'Wha-a-a-a-at'. Imagine if we spoke to each other in the same room. Now that would be pretty civilised.

Imagine if we stopped saying to our teenagers 'How can you call that music?' and they stopped saying to us 'That classical junk is so boring.' We could turn the volume down. We could use headphones. We could respect each other's right to listen to the sounds of our choice. Notice I could only bring myself to use the word 'sounds'. I am not that civil yet!

Imagine saying, in a calm and civilised fashion to your outlandishly garbed adolescent 'I wonder if you would mind looking in the mirror and checking that that is the image you wish to present.' Imagine if she did look in the mirror and said 'Mummy darling, I have reviewed my appearance and, while respecting your right to another opinion, I find it entirely delightful.' Now, that's going a bit too far!

I got a bit stuck on how to get around saying 'Sit up straight at the table and eat your peas . . . well at least try them. You don't have to like them, you just have to eat them,' in a manner that matched the spirit of civility.

Luckily, I re-read the article and extracted the second half of a sentence, completely out of context, that said, 'Civility is usually directed towards people one hardly knows or does not know at all.' After all, we parents need the best excuses we can find.

— *East & Bays Courier*

Grizzling is great

MOST MOTHERS REGARD LISTENING as part of our role. When our children come home from school, we listen empathically to all the small, unpleasant incidents of their day. We do this because we know that our children will feel better having got that off their chests and will, therefore, be able to get on with the important things in life like afternoon TV, tormenting younger siblings and avoiding homework.

When our husbands, hopefully one at a time, come home, we listen empathically about the awfulness of their day, the irritations they have encountered, the impossible people they have had to deal with, the deadlines that haven't been met due, of course, to someone else's failings.

We do this in the hope that, by the time they have got all that off their chest, by the time the kids have had a family meal and done their homework, by the time we have tucked into bed everyone shorter — and taller — than us, that we can manage two and a half minutes quality time together before total exhaustion sets in.

And who listens to us? Other mothers, of course. I don't think I could have survived, nor continue to survive, without the support of my (also mothers) friends. We do listen to each other and we do problem-solve together.

The problem is, we tend to use our time together to solve problems and there never seems to be time left over to grizzle. Grizzling is good for our health. Grizzling gets things off our chests.

Sometimes I just want to grizzle. I don't need a solution — just an ear.

Today I want to grizzle about the way in which I am the only one in this household who sees 'the big picture'. All my family are 'little picture' people. They know how to empty dishwashers, put washing on the line, hang up towels in the bathroom, even cook meals if pushed. They are, in fact, obliging people who will do almost anything I ask.

What they don't understand, however, is The Sequence. It's just great that they bring their baked beans bowls from the table, rinse them and put them in the dishwasher. But if they leave half the baked beans in the sink, the person who lives with the sink all day will have to dig for the sink by herself.

It's just great that they know where spare loo rolls are and can even replace them in emergency situations, but I no longer need the 'inners' saved for craft-work since the youngest left kindergarten seven years ago. So why store them behind the loo? The person who lives in the house all day can only stand the Craft Collection for just so long.

It's just great that they know how to soak clothing that requires hand-washing and even know how to add detergent and keep violent colours separate. Just what is it they think that I am going to use for the next three days for *my* gear?

The list goes on. Natural consequences are a bit hard to apply. Calling them out of a lecture and asking them to come home immediately to get their sleeping bag out of the hall where it was only airing for a few days seems churlish and does not do a great deal for harmony and good-will in the family.

So there's only one thing to do and that's Grizzle. I just hope someone out there is listening.

— *East & Bays Courier*

Pocket money

MANY OF YOU WILL already know that Barbara Coloroso has been to Auckland. She came to promote her book *Kids Are Worth It*, subtitled 'Giving your child the gift of inner discipline'.

I have enjoyed much of her wisdom and even tried out some of her ideas. As always happens in books on child rearing, the outcome is never quite as the book promises.

One of the themes in this book is 'pocket money'. I have always been a believer that children should not be paid for chores but should do them as part of the family. But where does that leave pocket money?

According to Barbara, the purpose of pocket money (allowance, if you are American) is to give children the experience of managing money. She suggests that you begin as soon as the child is old enough not to eat the coins, so we were pretty confident that Deborah's tenth birthday was a good time to start!

Further, she suggested, that whatever amount you gave your child, she should have some to save, some to spend and some to give away. The latter, we gathered, was for charitable purposes rather than to employ a neighbour to make your bed!

Although Barbara had recommended that the distribution be left entirely to the child we were not game for this, so we settled upon three dollars per week — fifty cents for each department and the balance to be used as she saw fit.

The effect was spectacular. A wave of agreeableness swept over me. No more 'We're not made out of money' speeches, no more ecological impossibilities — 'Do you think money grows on trees?' Instead, I agreed to everything.

'Let's all go to McDonald's, my shout,' suggested Deborah. 'Certainly,' we agreed. A hasty retreat to count the assets — this was, after all, the first week on the new system — followed by a small voice, saying, 'I don't think I'm that hungry.'

'My school tie doesn't hang too well, I'd like a new one,' suggested Deborah. 'Certainly,' said Mother. 'For that, I would be happy to subsidise 50:50, so why don't I help you look up the number of the Uniform Shop and you can find out the price.' Matter dropped.

'I really would like a new CD,' asked Deborah. 'Certainly,' said Mother. 'Next time we're near a music shop we'll just pop in and find out the price of a CD. Then you'll know how much you are up for.'

'I hate pocket money,' said Deborah.

Great system, Barbara.

— East & Bays Courier

Memory training

YOU KNOW WHAT IT is like. A parenting principle floats through your mind. You decide to take a stand. You stick to your guns. The cost (in terms of energy) to you is enormous. You may win the battle. But there is always the niggling doubt. 'Was it worth it?'

Well, that's what happened in our place last week.

A note came home from the jazz ballet class. 'Would we please send in the fees for the impending exam.' I was in a rare but impressive mood and wrote out the cheque immediately. That bit was simple. The tricky bit was going to be remembering to take it to class seven days hence.

A parenting principle — well several actually — flashed to mind. 'Whose problem is it? Give your child the opportunity to learn responsibility. Don't be your child's memory. Don't nag'. Clearly this was a Teachable Moment.

'Here's the cheque, darling.' She was on instant alert. She knows that 'darling' means that Mum is going to say something really ghastly but say it very nicely. 'Now how about putting it in a good place so that you remember to take it next week.'

The child has more brains than to fall for that one. 'I'll never remember. You keep it and you remember,' she rejoined. 'No, darling,' (two darlings in a row reveals maternal desperation) 'this one is your department.'

She threw down the gauntlet. 'I'm too little for that sort of responsibility.' Beware! Any ten-year-old who can throw a statement like that at you is ready, but definitely unwilling. We eyed each other, breathing heavily.

'Why don't you put it in your ballet shoe so you can't possibly forget it?' I suggested. 'I'll put it on my mirror,' she stated firmly. Now I know full well that when you put anything on your mirror, in a bid to remember it, it becomes transparent after two days and you never see it again. I offer this piece of wisdom. 'I'll put it on my mirror,' she said.

It was a dreadful week for me. Worrying about a child's memory is hard work. Keeping my mouth zipped was even harder. She was completely unconcerned and slept well each night.

The great day dawned. Would she remember? Should I interfere? Could I help myself?

She came home from school. She got changed. 'Why don't you brush your hair?' I hinted. She did but failed to see *you know what*. 'Look again in the mirror, you've missed a few strands of hair.' Now I call that subtle. It was. So subtle that she redid her hair, looking in the mirror, but still didn't see the cheque.

We got in the car. We got half way there. 'Mum, I forgot the cheque. Please can we go back?' I hope you are all very proud of me that I confined myself to a 'Sorry there isn't time'. It took enormous strength on my part to refrain from delivering my usual lecture that begins 'If only…'

Later that week she addressed an envelope and posted it.

The real question is not 'Did she learn from it?' The real question is 'Did I learn from it?' The test will come the next time we need a jazz ballet cheque. That could be several months away.

You will recognise me easily. I'll be the mother rushing up to the teacher to give her the money on the spot. I'm certainly not putting myself through another week like that again.

— *East & Bays Courier*

Let's take time out

WHEN OUR CHILDREN BEHAVE badly, when they hit, throw things, try to throw themselves off the changing table, won't leave the baby or the pot plant alone, we often send them to their room.

Time Out starts in our head
Decide which behaviours you are not prepared to tolerate. Start with the ones that hurt. No biting. No hair pulling. No pinching. No shoving. Then add in the ones that you need to do several times a day. Lie still while you have your nappy changed. Hold still while I help you dress.

Time Out is not a punishment
If we say, 'If you hurt the baby, you will go to Time Out', this makes it look like our child has a choice. She can choose to hurt the baby and then take the punishment. This is not what we want. We want a child who has decided not to hit.

Your child knows she is wrong
Imagine that I could interview your child.
    Diane: 'Are you allowed to hit the baby?'
    Child: (looking rather sheepish) 'No.'
    Diane: 'Do you hit the baby sometimes?'

Child: (looking somewhat rueful) 'Yes.'

This child fully understands that she is not allowed to hit the baby. There is no need to explain or warn.

When is a child old enough for discipline?

Your child is old enough for discipline when she is old enough to give you *'the look'*. Some children start as soon as they can crawl. Others may get close to eighteen months.

Picture the scene. There is a pot plant. Your toddler looks at the front, the back, sniffs the leaves, tests the leaves for taste, bendiness and strength. She runs her fingers through the soil. She is focused on what she is doing. This is normal exploratory behaviour for a toddler.

Now picture the other scene. Same pot plant. Same smell, taste and texture test. This time she is keeping a cheekily smiling or a challenging eye on you. Her face says, 'I know I am not supposed to be doing this.'

You have just experienced *'the look'*.

Time Out for tots

The lightest form of Time Out is when you simply get preoccupied and wait.

You want your child in her highchair. She says 'No' and runs to the other side of the kitchen, waiting to play chasey or to struggle and back-arch.

You quietly get on with something else. Pretty soon you hear a little voice saying 'Up, up.' Your little one has changed her mind and is ready to do as you asked.

Scoop and dump

Our child walks past the toddler and pushes him. We scoop her up and pop her in her room. There is no need to explain. She knows why she is there. We know why she is there. What is there to discuss?

When you reach the doorway, say, 'You know you are not allowed to shove the baby.' Once we have said that, there is very little else to add. Walk out saying, 'I'll be back to see if you are ready to behave.'

Children need space to struggle with themselves
You ask your two-year-old to hold still while you put her shoes on. She doesn't want her shoes on. As you approach her she begins kicking and flailing. You risk losing teeth.

Scoop her up and pop her in her cot or her room. Say, 'I'll be back to see if you are ready to have your shoes on.'

Walk out and wait about ten to fifteen seconds. Go back and ask 'Are you ready now?' More often than not, you have made your point and your child will accept a cuddle on the way down to the ground and then be ready to co-operate.

If not, you can go away for a bit longer knowing that your child is safe, coming to terms with the fact that you have asked for something to be done and that nothing much else is happening in her life until she is willing to do that.

But I want her to feel good about her cot
Any spot where she is safe and cannot get out of is fine. I favour a cot because it is safe and it is easy on my back.

When I put my toddler to sleep in her cot, I am warm, soothing and loving. 'It's time for a lovely sleep. Good night Daddy, good night teddy, goodnight mobile. Kiss for Mummy. Sleep tight.'

When my toddler is being deliberately obstructive or cheekily defiant, I scoop her up and pop her in her cot. It may look like the same place, but *my* behaviour is so different, that it feels different to my child.

If you have any concerns about using a cot or bedroom, a pushchair, a corner, a step — any safe spot will do. Time Out is not a room or a cot. Time Out is an attitude that you take.

But she keeps coming out
Clearly, she doesn't believe you when you tell her to stay there. You are going to have to convince her that, when you say 'Go to your room until you are ready' (to do as asked), you really do mean it.

Take her to her room and shut the door. Tie it to the next door or install a small bolt high up.

You only need to be this powerful when your child has already shown that she has no respect for your instruction to stay in her room.

A story from home
When Deborah was about eighteen months, we were over visiting her beloved Grandma. I have no idea what I did to annoy her, but she swiped at me — and connected. I was stunned and hurt and I remember racing her off and dumping her in my mother's laundry, shouting, 'You never hit a Mummy. Never! Ever! Ever!' and stalking out.

About half a minute later, I remembered all the advice I give to parents about making sure that Time Out is a safe place. I had scooped her up and dumped her in a place with Grandma's cactus collection and Grandma's detergent collection.

I went back in to find her standing, stunned, on the spot where I had left her. Clearly the speed and ferocity of my action had impressed her and she has never attempted to hit me again.

However, could you please, please make sure that *you* choose a Time Out spot that is safe for your child!

— Littlies

Let's avoid food wars

IT IS EASY TO be the mother of a child who enjoys food. Your little one opens his mouth like a hungry starling. The food you offer is eaten with obvious pleasure. The bottom of the plate appears within view. You get to use phrases like 'all gone'. Everyone thinks you are doing a good job.

But what if his response to a spoon is to turn his head away? What if your child is naturally slight? What if your child has little interest in food? Under these circumstances, the pressure on us is enormous and we often feel like bad mothers.

Some children don't care that much about food.

Our first two children, Robert and Tanya, were both keen on food. They ate what I put in front of them — though I must confess that was partly because I was very well trained to give them food they liked!

Our third child, Deborah, was really different. Sometimes she would eat lots and demand more. Other times, she would have a few mouthfuls and then, that would be it. Not another speck of food would pass her lips. 'Just one more spoon for Mummy' had no effect whatsoever.

How I learned not to have food battles
One morning, when Deborah was about two, it was morning tea-time.

I had put in front of her a plate of mandarin segments, toast cubes and cheese cubes. She scoffed down the mandarin and some of the toast and cheese and then asked to get down from her highchair.

I had read somewhere that, if a child didn't finish her plate, it should be saved till the next meal so that the child learned not to waste food. That made sense to me. I was not going to raise a picky child who wasted food. Water only — yes — but nothing more until that was eaten.

If mother was made of stern stuff, Deborah was made of sterner stuff. She held out on water only. Robert (15) and Tanya (13) would come to me privately and say 'Are you sure you know what you are doing?' I would go off and cry in my bedroom.

I couldn't bear it that she would eat dried out old toast that was set like concrete and cheese that was so dry that it had caved sides and split, so, whenever she was asleep or not looking, I would replace them with fresh cubes.

Deborah held out for thirty-six hours on water only. Then she ate. I had won — but it was a very hollow victory. But I had learned a lesson. I resolved that I would never engage in a food battle again.

So, what do you do with a picky eater?
The first thing is to change your thinking. Give up on thinking, 'How on earth am I going to get food into him today?' or 'What could I possibly prepare that he would like enough to finish?' This puts huge pressure on you to come up with the right trick or the right food.

Instead, start by thinking, 'It is a mother's job to offer her child access to reasonable amounts of food that he sort-of likes five times a day. What he does with this opportunity is his business.'

The plan
Begin at breakfast time. Put out a small quantity of the breakfast food you know your child likes. Ask him if he would like to be fed or if he would prefer to feed himself.

When he has had enough — even if it is nothing! — allow him to get down from his high-chair or leave the table. Cover the food. Keep it available. He may have it whenever he wishes — in the high-chair or at the table. However, if he wishes to eat different food, he will need to wait till morning tea-time.

At morning tea-time, quietly and without comment, dispose of any remaining breakfast food.

Morning tea

Put out a small quantity of morning tea food. It is fine to include a couple of biscuits or any other junk food along with the healthy food and, of course, your child will eat junk food first.

Remember that you are not trying to starve your child into eating food. You are merely offering a fresh eating opportunity about every two hours. This does not equate to torturing a child — even though your child may scream as if he has been.

When your child has lost interest in the food, he may leave the table, knowing that you will keep that food available till the next meal.

Repeat this pattern with each meal. An hour or two after dinnertime, the kitchen is closed.

Useful tips

Begin with very small quantities. Should he ask for more, you will find a way to cope.

Avoid foods touching each other. Particularly avoid an undesirable food touching a desirable food. Apparently the contamination renders all the good stuff uneatable. If I were dealing with a really fussy eater today, I would contemplate buying a Japanese bento box.

Juice and milk are liquid foods. If our children get a lot of their calories from liquid foods, we shouldn't be surprised that they have little appetite for solid foods.

Don't put up with appalling or even halfway bad behaviour just so your children will eat. If you allow your children to loll out of their chairs, mix it all together to make food soup, walk around with food, gaze at the TV while you spoon food into an absentminded mouth, you are giving your children a way of holding you hostage to their eating.

What to expect

Expect a lot of complaining for the first two days. Expect a pathetic little voice saying, 'I'm hungry' while having the opportunity of eating healthy food and wishing for chocolate biscuits.

Expect to feel greatly relieved of the burden of having to spend twenty-four hours a day thinking about what your child does or does not eat.

— *Littlies*

Night-time waking

SOME BABIES ARE EASYGOING and give in gracefully to our wish to sleep alone — or with another adult — all night. Others give us a very clear message that we are not meeting their needs and/or wants and we better hurry up and do it the baby's way or *there is going to be trouble.*

So what is a parent supposed to do if she chooses to have her babies and toddlers sleeping in their own bed all night?

Meet your baby's needs

Deborah was our third child. By the time she was born, I had the confidence to decide that only *she* really knew when she was hungry. Rather than try to make her stick to a timetable, I followed these principles by day:

- Hunger wakes a little baby out of sleep — feed her.
- After she is fed, a baby needs company and things to look at — keep her with you.
- When she is tired, put her to bed, kiss her tenderly, walk away.

One of the hardest habits to overcome was trying to get another feed in before I put her to sleep — on the basis that, if her tummy was full, she would sleep for longer.

If a baby or toddler drifts off to sleep while feeding, is patted off to sleep or always has a parent present when she goes to sleep, she learns that these are the conditions necessary for getting back to sleep when she surfaces in the middle of the night. Since a baby surfaces about every hour and since there are 1,825 parenting nights before a baby starts school, I figured that my baby did have to learn to go to sleep alone on a flat surface. It was not what she wanted and she did yell a lot and I did hate that. I would give her ten minutes with me at the other end of the house and it was amazing how often she fell asleep after nine minutes and thirty seconds.

By night, I had fewer principles:

- Hunger wakes a little baby out of sleep — feed her.
- Put her to bed.

These worked well quite often — but not all the time. Nothing ever does, in parenting.

As she grew older, we discovered that her preference was not to sleep through the night for more than two months in a row. Her regular good-sleep pattern was easily disrupted by a cold, a tooth, a measle or a mump, so we constantly had to re-convince her.

We used three methods, with varying degrees of success, to re-train her when she had lost the knack of going off to sleep.

Cold turkey

We followed a standard bath, drink, teeth clean (when she had teeth!), story, kiss good night routine and then we left. If we needed to attend to her in the middle of the night, we did everything the same except for bath, drink, teeth, story. In other words, we walked in, ascertained that this was a situation of *want* rather than *need*, kissed her good night and walked out.

She did not appreciate this fine method and she was very noisy in her lack of appreciation. It always took three pretty horrible nights and then she slept — until the next time.

The best bit of comfort and advice I can give you is 'listen to the crying'. If you are getting yelling and then a gap, yelling and then a gap, you are going in the right direction. She can stop (our biggest fear is that our child is unable to stop crying), listen to see if anyone is going to change their minds, and then start up again. *She can stop.*

Settling at increasing intervals

Dr Christopher Green in his book *Toddler Taming* talks about going in after five, ten, fifteen etc minutes, assuring your child that you are there and you love her, and walking out. His belief is that this gives the child the security of knowing that you are there and so that child can go off to sleep.

I often ask parent groups I speak to how many of them have used this method. Almost everybody has tried. When I ask them how many have been successful, about a third have. These are the babies who interpret their parents' behaviour the way Dr Green says they will.

I believe that the other two-thirds interpret their parents' behaviour as 'Ah ha! So the rule is that I have to cry at increasingly longer intervals and eventually a parent will come.'

The pop-in method

I was searching for a way to give Deborah, now sixteen months, recognition for getting it right, without actually shaking her awake and telling her she had gone off to sleep very nicely.

Any parent who has a child who can stay in bed for thirty seconds can use this method. Many clients have used it with enormous success — and it does not involve any crying (parent or child)!

- Kiss your child good night and tell her you will pop in to see how good she is being.
- Go back thirty seconds (no kidding — thirty seconds) later and tell her she is being 'so-o-o-o-o good'. Tell her you will pop in to see how good she is being.
- Go back a minute later and tell her she is being 'so-o-o-o-o good'. Tell her you will pop in to see how good she is being.
- Go back two minutes later and tell her she is being 'so-o-o-o-o good'. Tell her you will pop in to see how good she is being.

Keep increasing the interval by a minute until you go in to

find your child asleep with a smile on her face.

I found this hard work to be so self-disciplined as a parent, but it did work and it was by far the most pleasant method I ever used.

Years later, Deborah would still say 'Pop in, please, Mummy' when I tucked her in and kissed her good night. You don't get a better testimonial than that!

What about the child who keeps coming out?
We all know the feeling. We have bathed, pyjama-ed, cuddled, read stories, tucked in, kissed good night, walked out and felt mighty relieved that our parenting was over until the morning. Ten minutes later, so my mother told me, I would appear saying, 'My button's undone!' Your child may well appear with a different excuse — but it is nonetheless an excuse for being out of bed.

Don't ask, 'What are you doing here?' because you really aren't interested in the reason. Your parenting day is over. Scoop up your little darling, pop her in her bed, say firmly, 'If you come out again, the door will be shut.'

If she comes out again — and she will — scoop her up, put her in her bed and say, 'You came out. Your door will be shut for five minutes.'

After five minutes, go back and offer her the opportunity to stay in bed with the door open. Most children prefer to have the door open and connecting them with the rest of the family.

If you have done this three times in a row, you are clearly being 'had'. I would close the door and leave the child to go off to sleep with the door shut.

A way of thinking
The best way I have found of thinking about my parenting job in night-time hours is 'Between the hours of 7.00 a.m. and 7.00 p.m. I am a lovely mother who attends to all of my child's needs and many of her wants. After 7.00 p.m. the mothering shop is closed!'

— *Littlies*

Do tell tales

MOST OF US HAVE the schoolyard words 'I'm telling on you' and 'Don't tell tales' still ringing in our ears. If you are of my vintage, you will remember the nasty little schoolyard ditty:

Tell-tale tit
Your tongue will split
And all the little puppy-dogs
Will have a little bit.

In a bizarre way, 'telling' was regarded as a bigger crime than hitting, shoving, being verbally nasty or damaging property.

When we were hurt and upset and went to the parent or teacher who, after all, was responsible for our well-being and began to pour out our tale of woe, we were often cut short with, 'I don't want to hear about it. Don't tell tales.'

And if we reported some unkind and hurtful words, we were often reminded:

Sticks and stones
Will break my bones
But words will never hurt me.

We can all remember how unhelpful and unsupportive this was and yet, when our own beloved child runs to us crying, 'Emma was mean to me', we often hear the same words coming out of our mouths.

Our children need our support
If our children are upset, they need a pair of loving arms around them, to help them deal with their feelings. Pick them up, give them a cuddle and say something along the lines of 'Oh sweetheart, how awful for you' — and say it with sincerity. Our children need to know we understand what it is like for them and that we really care.

Boring Cuddles are great
At this point, we often try to shorten the process and encourage our children not to make a fuss. This usually means that our children have to cry much harder to convince us they really are feeling upset!

I find that the fastest and easiest way to get our children back on an even keel is just to hold them still — sitting down makes it a lot easier — and say nothing much more. This Boring Cuddle (i.e. no more words, no entertainment) gives them comfort and support without our getting involved in the problem. Pretty soon, they will wriggle to get down and either go back happily into the same situation or decide to go someplace else.

Either way, our child has solved the problem with a little support and no intervention on our part.

But I want to help
Because we love our children and we really do care, we often get hooked into tackling the problem for them.

We blame: 'What did you do to Emma?'

We criticize: 'Why can't you two just play nicely together?'

We distract: 'Don't think about it. I'll help you find something else to do.'

We explain: 'You are so lucky to have such a nice little girl to play with.'

We lecture: 'You won't have friends if you run off crying to Mum all the time.'

We problem-solve: 'How about you ride your bikes together?'

It is a long, exhausting process, which sometimes works and sometimes doesn't and often results in our getting exasperated and exhausted and muttering 'Why don't you just go to your room and sulk?'.

It is so much easier just to offer comfort and support and let our child solve the problem.

What about the offender?
Our child has been in a tricky situation and done something very, very sensible. They got out of the situation and ran to safety: a perfect solution. They have assertively shown the other child that they do not intent to stay around and be treated badly.

Unless there are blood, bruises or teeth-marks, there is nothing else that we need to do.

Won't all this cuddling make my child a cry-baby?
What makes our children whingy and whiny is when we do the work of solving the problems, thinking up alternatives, arguing with them that it was nowhere near as bad as they thought, and telling them that they shouldn't have run to us in the first place. They wind up having to whinge a lot more to convince us of their cause.

I have found that the ability to run to an adult who offers comfort and support but no solution makes our children brave and competent. We are relying on them — with a little bit of non-verbal help from us — to be able to solve the problem and decide what to do next.

Let's get informed and relaxed
When our child rushes to us distressed, it gives us a wonderful opportunity. We get to assess if it is an emergency or a minor upset. We get to decide whether intervention is necessary or unnecessary. We get to listen and to comfort.

And we — as exhausted parents — don't need to do anything more than mutter some soothing sound and give a Boring Cuddle. It seems a fair trade to me!

— Littlies

Is smacking the answer?

Diane, have you smacked?
Thirty-one years ago, I was confident that a small, light smack was the answer. When my child would reach for the pot plant, the precious item, the hot object, I had a plan. I would kindly, but firmly, say 'No! (name not yet known). Leave that alone, please. It is dangerous/fragile/unsuitable.' If that didn't stop him or if he came back for another try, I would repeat what I had said, but more firmly. One more time and I would administer a small smack to the back of the outstretched hand and that would be that. My child would learn not to repeat the action.

Two years later, I had a *real* eighteen-month-old. The theory didn't seem to work with him. One smack would make Robert irritated, a second would make him upset, a third would make him furious, upset and grimly determined. None of the smacks seemed to help him change his mind.

Our second child was different. She liked to be good and stay out of trouble. Of course there were days when her behaviour deteriorated. If she got seriously out-of-hand, one smack and she would cry for half an hour, sleep for two hours (which was probably the problem in the first place) and then behave well for a number of weeks.

Our third child was the most strong-willed of all. By this time, I had been a Family Therapist for a number of years and had a lot more skills. However, sooner or later, I would become sufficiently desperate/annoyed/despairing to resort to smacking. For Deborah, this meant that she felt entitled to be resentful and angry and plot revenge.

So the answer is 'Yes! I have smacked.' Do I recommend it as a method of discipline? No. Let me explain.

There is a limit to how many times you can smack

You ask your child to put a few blocks away. She doesn't want to. You offer her a smack. She opts for the smack and then says, 'That didn't hurt.' You produce a smack that does. Her eyes water but she holds her ground and says 'I'm still not going to do it.' You smack once more. She cries, but she is still not going to do it.

At this point, one of two things may happen. One, we lose our temper and wind up smacking or hitting much harder than we intended. Most parents find this dreadfully upsetting. Our child is distraught (possibly crying in her room), we are distraught (possibly crying in our room). The blocks are doing fine. They are just sitting there.

At the end of an episode like this it is unlikely that we would have the heart to go back and insist that she picks up seven blocks.

You give up

The other option, having smacked a couple of times, is that we don't have the heart to continue. We just cannot bear to smack any more. We feel discouraged. Our child may feel unhappy or feel she has won. The blocks still sit there. The atmosphere is awful.

But, it worked for my parents

Smacking worked a lot better in the times that when a parent smacked, she had the backing of the State, the Church and the police. It worked at a time when it was horrific for a child to hit back at a parent.

We live in a different era. Our children see violence day in, day out on television, as part of computer games and on the big screen. They see violence portrayed as the simplest way to force your own way or opinion on anyone — and to be the hero or heroine.

We live in such violent times that it behoves us to model, to our children, ways of resolving issues other than hitting.

We are the role model
Whether we want to or not, we are a role model to our children. They learn their good behaviour and they learn their bad behaviour through watching ours. It is hard for them to escape the lesson that, if you don't fancy someone's behaviour, the way to deal with it is through smacking them.

One of my favourite cartoons shows a father paddling a son while saying 'That will teach you not to hit other people.'

Smacking is not a good look
Today, I think of so many better ways I could have dealt with situations other than smacking. Certainly, I could have behaved better than the yelling and screaming that preceded and accompanied most smacking in our household.

I learned something else about smacking. Vernon and I were, and are, loving and caring parents. In 'the smacking days' we probably used smacking about equally. I learned that when *I* was the one doing the smacking it felt more-or-less OK. When I listened to Vernon doing the smacking it felt horrible and, definitely, when I see an unknown parent in the supermarket swiping at a child's legs or bottom, it just looks like a larger person hitting a smaller person.

Last word about smacking
As we leave the subject of smacking, I will leave the last word to Robert. This story happened when he was about four.

At one desperate stage, I stormed at him, 'You're going to get a good hiding.' His response was, 'There is no such thing as a *good* hiding.' He was right, but it probably didn't save him that day!

— *Littlies*

Building self-esteem in toddlers

PICTURE THE SCENE:

You take your toddler to a new playground. There is a slide there with four steps up and a nice gentle gradient. You help your child to climb up the steps, grip the rails to sit down and then slide down. The first few times he goes slowly and cautiously. As his confidence grows he needs less and less help. Pretty soon all you have to do is sit on the park bench and keep a safety eye out.

He has the odd stumble and gets the occasional fright. He may need to rush over for a quick hug. Back he goes, chuckling with delight at his own cleverness and delighting in his own mastery. He has tackled something that he initially found challenging and practised it until he had it mastered. He has discovered that wonderful heady feeling of 'I can.'

He is on the path to high self-esteem.

Mister Clingy

There is a second child at the same playground. He is gripping his Dad's hand and whinging. Dad is encouraging him to have a go at climbing the steps, but he won't have a bar of it. He buries his head in Dad's shoulder and points at the swing. Dad obediently takes him over to the swing and stands there for ages pushing it. When Dad suggests a change of activity, the child cries and whines and demands that Dad keeps on pushing the swing.

He demands Dad does exactly as he says. He doesn't test himself with a new activity, he quells his natural curiosity and doesn't get the thrill of mastery. He behaves as if 'he can't'. He's not much fun to take to the playground.

Dad worries about his self-esteem.

Over-the-hill-and-far-away
There is a third child at the same playground — well not exactly *at* the playground. He hopped out of the car and started running. His Mum is trying to keep up and to keep him safe. He looks back occasionally and laughs at her. He is heading for big-kid swings and risks getting bowled. His behaviour is dangerous and getting out-of-control.

He doesn't get a chance to master the slide. He's too busy creating havoc. He, too, is not much fun to take to the playground.

He's bright and bubbly and no one is worrying about his self-esteem just yet. As he gets older he is harder to manage and his parents wonder about how he is going to go at school when he will be required to follow directions.

Later, they will worry about his ability to focus and worry about things he just can't seem to manage.

What is high self-esteem about?
People, of all ages, with high self-esteem have confidence without arrogance. They know that there are many things that they *can* do. They are curious to find out about new things and to test themselves. They are willing to tolerate the ordinary frustrations of life and to try things that they find difficult. They delight in their own and others' achievements.

What is low self-esteem about?
Low self-esteem increases when we convince ourselves that difficult things are too hard and we give up on attempting to try new things or tolerating ordinary frustrations. We convince ourselves, and others around us, that we *can't*. Often, we really mean that we *won't*.

How can I help my 'Mr Clingy'?

Often, we put a lot of effort into persuading, cajoling, bribing and explaining. Our child resists our offers and we wind up feeling exhausted, frustrated and worried. The fastest way to help our child get over his anxieties is to be warmly supportive but unhelpful. A 'boring cuddle' is great. Sit with an arm around your child and let him watch and assess the situation. Don't distract him with encouragement.

Pretty soon, he will hop down and go near or even have a go. He may rush back for a top-up cuddle and, if you are supportive but boring — no words, he will take off again. He is moving from '*I can't*' to '*I can*'.

What about my 'runaway'?

We are often convinced that these children cannot hold still while we dress them, cannot walk next to us holding our hand, cannot see a younger child without exuberantly squeezing them in a bear hug, cannot see a couch without having to bounce on it.

We need to start with ourselves and change our thinking from '*they can't*' to '*they won't*'. Once *we* are convinced that they are capable but unwilling, we can stop accepting their '*I won't*' and move to '*You have to*'.

Let's start at home where we have maximum control of the situation. If your toddler back-arches and wriggles when you lie him back to change his nappies, pop him in his cot till he is ready to co-operate. If he runs around and won't let you dress him, keep him in his room until he is ready to hold still and co-operate.

Each time he *begins* to move from gentle hug to 'squeeze like lemon', scoop him up and pop him in a quiet spot till he is ready to be gentle. Stop him every time he treats furniture like a trampoline. When our child can behave well indoors, the odds are they will be less inclined to behave dangerously outdoors.

Allowing our children to behave badly is the same as giving them permission. Once our children are convinced that we won't give them permission to behave badly, they and we will be convinced that they *can* behave appropriately.

High self-esteem

Natural reserve is very attractive in a child and we do not want to take it away. We need to support our children to overcome excessive caution to try new things, enjoy new experiences and master new situations. Discovering that they *can* overcome their natural caution when it is appropriate, leads them to have quiet confidence in their own abilities. In other words, high self-esteem.

Lively exuberance is also a very attractive quality and we don't want to quell natural enthusiasm. However, when our children's behaviour is inappropriately unrestrained, it is our job to help them exercise suitable restraint so that they can be pleasant to be with and so we can enjoy their company without worrying about what they will get up to next. Discovering that they *can* exercise restraint and behave well gives them the quiet inner confidence that leads to high self-esteem.

And there is no doubt that having curious, enthusiastic, well-mannered children who are a pleasure to be with, is great for parental self-esteem!

— *Littlies*

Disciplining other people's children

ANOTHER CHILD, NOT YOUR own, pushes your child away from the slide so that she can get up first, a two-year-old snatches the rattle off your baby, a small visitor insists on walking around your house with a glass of bright orange juice, a visiting child asks very politely to watch a video while all the other children have been sent outside to play, a little troupe of four-year-olds (yours included) start running around in circles in your living room. What can you do, what should you do, what are you allowed to do?

Disciplining other people's children is much trickier than tackling our own. If we do have to reprimand or deal in some way with someone else's child, we always want to do it in such a way as not to offend the other parent, who may well be a very dear friend.

It is very hard to find ourselves with adult friends whose company we really enjoy — but their children are badly behaved and a nightmare to have in our home. (By the way, it is not much fun being the parent of a very difficult child and to realise that the daytime invitations are petering out and we are starting to get invited solely to 'grown-ups only' events.)

In our home: Mum not there
When we are in our home supervising other people's children, we have full rights and responsibility to protect all the children and our

property. The worst that we risk is that the child may report back that 'Diane was mean' or 'Diane was growly'. Hopefully, the parent will ask what Diane growled about and be none too impressed with 'She didn't like it when I took the truck away from James.'

It is much easier to front up to other people's children and demand reasonable behaviour when there is no adult audience. We simply treat the child as if they were our own, the household rules apply to everybody, with the exception that we never smack someone else's child and rarely shout at them.

It is much harder, however, when you have another parent present who is feebly saying, 'Don't do that, darling. It isn't nice. Now look, you've made him unhappy', or, worse still, making a point of not even looking in the direction where the mayhem is happening.

So what can we do in front of another child's parent so that we are containing the situation without being offensive to the parent?

Get up and go over
The hardest bit is deciding to do something about it. It is always easier to stop a situation before it escalates, but we have to overcome our eternal hope that 'If I don't notice it, maybe it will go away.' Most of the time, 'Just ignore the behaviour and it will stop,' is appealing but totally inaccurate advice.

We cannot deal with children by remote control. It simply doesn't work to sit in our chair and bleat, 'Will you kids just behave,' or to sit there and shout, 'Will you kids cut it out!' Believe me, they won't.

The first step is to get up. If you say to the other parents, 'Excuse me. I'll just go and deal with it,' you have committed yourself to action. Go over to the child who is misbehaving and stand right next to them. Often that is all that is needed to stop the behaviour — a parent (not your own) showing up, getting in close and looking stern.

Rules of the house
Rather than tell a particular child to do something or to stop doing something, we are much more powerful — and much less likely to offend the mother — if we begin what we have to say with 'The rule

of this house is . . .' or 'In this house we . . .' That way, it isn't personal to one child.

It is very hard for either parent or child to feel aggrieved at the MOTH (Mother Of The House) declaring:

- The rule in this house is that we are kind to younger children.
- In this house, we only have drinks sitting down in the kitchen.
- The rule in this house is that we play with balls outside.
- The rule here is that you don't snatch toys when someone is playing with them.
- It's a lovely day and everybody is playing outside for a while.
- NO running with sticks allowed.

Confident expectation

Stand there, looking absolutely confident and determined that your household rules will be followed. Most of us who are gentler souls find this quite difficult to do. The only thing I can think of to encourage us is that experience shows that if we don't get in early and stop the behaviour, it is only going to get worse. If you don't feel that strong, *fake it*. The children won't be able to tell the difference.

Some things are too precious

There will often, particularly for our sensitive children, be particular toys that are special and precious and our children will feel unable to share. It is a good idea, before the hordes descend, to ask your child, 'Which are your special toys that you don't want to share. Let's put them in a box and I'll put them safely away.' This is a way of being respectful to our child while showing clearly that we expect sharing.

Our fear is that our child will demand that his entire room be packed up and put in storage. Not so. I have found that this respectful approach usually means that our child will carefully pick out those things he cannot possibly bear to share and be able to handle quite graciously the sharing of the remainder.

Kiwi hospitality

We have strange rules of hospitality when it comes to children sharing toys. When children come around to our place to play, we tend to say, 'Now James! You're the host. You need to share your toys nicely and let the other children play with them.' As we go to someone else's house, we often lecture, 'Now James! We are going to Fergus' house. You are the guest and it would be polite to play what Fergus wants to play.'

When you think about it, that means that James never gets to play with his toys or play the games he wants to play.

Sharing systems
Some children just seem to play nicely together. Others need a bit of adult support to make things fair and equitable. When there is one preferred toy and two or more children, we may need a system. In any case, teaching our children that it is possible to use a fair system for sharing means they can generalise the concept to all sorts of other situations.

Many games, today, come with an old-fashioned egg timer. If not, buying one is one of the better, cheaper pieces of parenting paraphernalia that you can buy.

Teach your children to take turns and to give up their turn when the sand runs out. For a start, you may need to help them decide who goes first and you may need to help them 'give up' the treasured possession when the time runs out. It is amazing how quickly children can learn a system that is transparent and fair.

Who knows! On another occasion, you may even hear them say, 'In our house, the rule is your turn lasts until the sand runs out!'

— *Littlies*

Bribes, incentives and rewards

BRIBES, INCENTIVES AND REWARDS are all parenting strategies that I have used. Let's add persuaded, cajoled, warned, threatened and shamelessly used the spirit of competition.

'Let's have a race to see who can be first out of the bath?'

'Just hold still while I change you and then we can have a story.'

'If you keep running around the bathroom while I am trying to dry you, there'll be no TV.'

'Come on darling, just three more mouthfuls and you can have yummy ice-cream.'

'If we leave the park right now, we'll be home in time to see Daddy.'

I've used them all. Some of them worked well. Some of them didn't. Some of them worked three times, but not the fourth. Some of them made my life simpler and some of them came back to haunt me.

So should we use bribes, incentives and rewards or should we abandon them?

Bribery, incentive or reward?

Is 'just hold still while I change you and then we can have a story' a bribe, an offer of reward for effort or just a pleasant way of parenting a co-operative child? The answer lies in whether we *have* to do it or not to get compliance.

If it is just one of those pleasant, chatty things we say on the way to get changed, if our child co-operates and then we enjoy a story together, there is free will on both sides and a good time is had by all.

If it means that our child does something that they find rather difficult with a minimum of fuss and then we recognize the effort involved, it seems a perfectly reasonable way of making life a little easier.

However, when we open our negotiations with an offer, 'If you will do . . . , then I will . . . ,' we are not only trying to bribe our children into compliance, we are also, quite inadvertently, giving them a choice. 'If you just hold still while I change you, we can have a lovely story.' All they have to do is say, 'No thanks, Mum. I don't feel like a story.' It may be true or it may be a clever fake, and they don't have to get dressed either. Bribery only works as long as the child falls for the bribe.

When your child responds readily to an offer of a reward, when they heed your warning, when they energetically try to get a task done in the spirit of wholesome competition, we feel like successful parents. We set up a strategy and it worked. It made life easier and it was fun. Go for it.

If it's getting harder, pause and think
Sometimes our children 'wise up' and start to bargain with us.

Mum: 'Darling, if you get dressed quickly, we'll have time for a story.'

Child: 'No Mummy. I want two stories.'

Or

Child: 'No Mummy. A game *and* a biscuit.'

Our child is starting to raise the stakes. She has stopped engaging in complying with the help of a small incentive and begun to believe that, when Mum asks her to do something, it is time to open negotiations. She is moving along the path towards expecting a reward for ordinary compliance.

We may be starting to feel our authority is a bit shaky. We are asking for something to be done and our child is beginning to think that there are entitlements to be had.

Our child is on her way to thinking the world owes her. These are warning signals.

D-Day — you're in trouble

The day we ask our child to do something and she demands to know what she will get, is D-Day. In this case, D-Day stands for Demand Day. You don't have to wait until this day, but if you get there, it is time to take action. She no longer believes that you do something because Mum or Dad ask you. She believes that you check the incentive and if it is adequate — in her opinion! — she may graciously or grumpily concede.

It is time for us to get a firm grip on our parenting attitude. We need to stop thinking 'What do *I* have to do to encourage my child to do as she is told' and start thinking 'As a parent, I am entitled to ask for simple things' like:

'Hold still while I dress you.'
'Get out of the bath now.'
'It's time to go home now.'
'It's time to sit up at the table and eat your dinner.'

And expect my child to do it simply because I asked.

Look ahead

If bribery isn't working for a child now, it is most unlikely to work later. Right now we are dealing in chocolate biscuits and stories. However, we may be on a pathway that leads to paying our children pocket money for ordinary chores, even for getting dressed. And many of us can remember from our school days the child whose parents offered, 'If you get good marks in Bursary, I'll buy you a car.' This is not a good pathway for us to be on.

Another way of looking at it — for the child who fusses about getting changed, or sitting at the table, or having to clean his teeth before bedtime, or some other ordinary childhood request — is to ask ourselves, 'How may times do you think he will need to clean his teeth between now and leaving high school?'

Looking ahead in this way tells us very clearly whether to proceed with rewards, threats and bribery, or whether we need to go with 'When a parent asks a child to do something, that is what is happening next.'

So, what's the alternative?

But how do we keep from heading off in the negative direction of bribery becoming a way of life? There are alternatives to our children doing things because we offer bribes, incentives and rewards. They could do it just because we asked them.

Make sure that there are plenty of times in the day when you ask for something to be done without even a hint of reward or consequence. Doing as told is an important step on the way to our children becoming self-disciplined adults. Expect your child to do as told, simply because you have asked.

Writing articles is such an exhausting business. I think I deserve a cup of coffee and some chocolate biscuits!

— Littlies

Sibling mayhem

I'VE ALWAYS FANCIED THE term 'Sibling *Mayhem*' rather than 'Sibling *Rivalry*'. 'Sibling Mayhem' implies that the moment you have more than one child, you can expect a certain amount of chaos just because there is more than one child in the room. Three young children and one digger-bucket can almost guarantee a high degree of mayhem.

The reason I don't like the term 'Sibling Rivalry' is that it implies that, just because people are siblings, rivalry is compulsory. Rivalry for what? Rivalry for parents' attention, which leads us to believe that the reason our children fight and squabble is that they are not getting enough parental attention.

I really disagree with this. Most of our children are getting more than enough parental attention, certainly more than their parents or grandparents ever did. And most parents are working tremendously hard to ensure that children get the attention that they need, the attention that they want — and then some.

So, why do children fight?
The simplest answer is, 'Because they can!' When we intervene, try to help sort it out, try to explain one child's position to another, try to offer alternative things to play with or alternative things to do, we may well sort out the immediate crisis, but we are also giving our children the message that it is their job to squabble and our job to sort it out.

I find that sorting out children's squabbles is very hard work and, once we start along the road of 'Now each of you are going to tell me what happened . . .', we wind up being Counsel for the Prosecution, Counsel for the Defence, Judge, Jury, and often the Executioner as well.

It is exhausting and frustrating work and not all of us set out to have a home-career in Law.

So, what are the alternatives?
We are usually dealing with one or several of these situations:

- There is a recurring squabble over a some desirable item.
- Children close in age.
- Wider age-gaps.
- Someone very upset comes running to us.
- We see unacceptable behaviour happening in front of us.
- We can hear the situation 'hotting up' in a different room.

Children close in age
Many of the disagreements when children are close in age is about the sharing of a toy or some other resource. There can be hideous battles over whose turn is it for the red chair, who gets to sit by the window in the car, who gets first go on the bike, how long is a turn.

Develop a system that looks fair to everyone. Although they are often a pain to set up and to monitor, systems not only save a lot of squabbles they also teach your children to develop their own systems of fairness.

Where there are issues over whose turn it is, the simplest way I know is to post a roster on the fridge showing — for all to see — whose day (under five 'whose day?' or over five 'whose week?') it is to go first at everything that happens that day.

Timers are great for making length of turns fair. An old-fashioned egg timer can be used from a very early age. Kitchen timers and stove timers work well for older children.

Wider age-gaps
Often we have to protect our preschoolers' construction games from

marauding toddlers. Rather than trying to get our toddlers to stop touching and eating small, irresistible pieces of Lego, it is easier to persuade our older children to play with these during the younger one's rest time or, at the very least, to play in the centre of a high desk or table.

Often we allow a preschooler to snatch a fancied toy off the baby, provided he quickly distracts the baby by replacing it. While this buys us peace at the time, we are teaching our preschooler that it is OK to take things provided the baby doesn't get upset. For long-term family harmony, insist that — if a baby has an appropriate toy in hand — he is allowed to play with it until he loses interest and lets go.

Someone comes running

By running to you, your child has already taken appropriate action. He has got out of the way of dangerous people and taken himself to a safe place. Other than saying something along the lines of 'You are really upset/hurt/angry', there is not much else that needs to be done. What he needs from you now is a cuddle and the ability to stay with you until he feels better. After he has settled down, he can decide for himself whether to return to the scene or play elsewhere.

But what about the perpetrator? Unless there is blood or teeth marks you don't need to do anything else just now. By all means ask what happened, but use it as useful information gathering rather than an obligation to go and sort it.

If this sort of thing is happening often, you need to get more vigilant so that you are more likely to catch the perpetrator in the act!

You see it happening

I am presuming that you have simple household rules, such as 'Don't hit, bite, snatch, pinch, shove or cuddle too tight.' If you see one child doing any of these, remove him from the scene and say very firmly, 'You know you are not allowed to hit/bite/pinch, etc. You are welcome back to play as soon as you are ready not to hit.'

Avoid getting into conversations about 'look how much you've upset your little sister' because that may have been his intention.

Also avoid 'How would you like it if someone hit/bit/pinched you?' Just now your child has very little interest in compassion.

By removing the child, you are making it very clear that you will not tolerate seeing another human being treated in this fashion.

You hear it hotting up
We have all heard a situation hotting up in another room and crept away, pretending that we haven't heard and hoping like crazy it would all go away. Then we hear the scream or the crash.

If you wish to teach your children that you don't condone fighting in your household, you need to get in early, just when you begin to hear the temperature rising.

Get in fast and break it up. 'Afternoon tea-time' is a sure winner. Asking for a task to be done is less popular but works just as well. Or you may choose simply to walk in, say 'This isn't working', and split the children into two separate rooms for about ten minutes.

If you do this every time your children fight and argue, the level of scrapping will drop considerably. Eventually, all you will have to do is approach 'heavy-footed' and the fighting will stop.

They may learn not to fight. They may learn to fight very quietly so that you don't interrupt. Either way, you have dealt effectively with Sibling Mayhem.

— Littlies

Coping with trauma, loss and grief

NO MATTER HOW WELL we look after our children and try to shield them from the 'rough stuff' of life, there will inevitably be times when they have to deal with losses and pain. At these times, even if there is nothing that we can do to make the immediate situation better, there are several things we can do to help our children get past the experience and integrate it into their lives.

Responses will vary
Children will react to trauma, loss and grief in a variety of ways and, just as with adults, there is no correct way for a child to respond. An outgoing, bubbly child may respond very dramatically with lots of loud crying and overt upset. They may well need to hear about what happened many, many times and have a need to tell everyone about the great event. A more reserved child may become quiet and thoughtful and go off and spend time alone integrating the information. Our strong-willed children may be very angry that this has happened, be outraged that it couldn't be prevented and seek to blame someone for it. And some children just take it in their stride and show very little response. All these are valid responses.

Tell the truth — tactfully
In our parents' day and certainly in our grandparents' day, children were shielded as much as possible from traumatic events and many people believed that, if you just didn't talk about it, a child would soon forget. As a response to our own childhood and the secrecy and denial that we experienced, we are often tempted to go to the other extreme and 'tell all' so that our children will never have to have the experience of someone disappearing from their life and then feeling that they cannot ask questions.

I believe that we should tell our children the facts as truthfully as we can, while being very aware that we shouldn't overload them with more information or more emotion than they can handle.

We also need to remember that children are very literal and it may not be altogether helpful to use euphemisms to shield them. (One of my more spectacular failures was trying to explain what happened at her uncle's funeral to my four-year-old. I was describing the burial — 'As they lowered his body into the ground'. She looked absolutely horrified, held her hand across her throat and said, 'Only his body! But what about his head?!')

Beloved pets
One of the earliest experiences of loss and death that our child may experience is the loss of a beloved pet. One of the nicest ways we can bring some comfort to our child, is to explain to him that, although Rover may not still be around to play with and to cuddle, his memory can still live on in the way we talk about him and remember all the lovely, funny and naughty things that he did.

Pet funerals, even though they may be very sad and accompanied by lots of tears, are a good way of helping our child deal with the reality of their loss and of honouring what their pet has meant to them. Some children like to pick a favourite toy (of the pet's) to be buried with it and they may like to add something of their own. Make a short speech about what the pet has meant to your family and invite your child to say something as well. Visiting the burial site, presumably at the end of your section, and putting some flowers there may give your child great comfort.

Losing grandparents

We may well have to deal, at the same time, with our own grief at losing a parent and our children's grief at losing a grandparent. This is one of the toughest parts of parenting, but our children are learning to cope with their own grief by watching us deal with theirs and ours. Don't be afraid to let them see how sad you are, but protect them from grief that absolutely overwhelms you. Children find it scary to see a parent completely out of control.

All families and cultures have different ideas about children attending funerals. For children under five, the length of time involved in a funeral may make it an impractical idea. At my late mother's funeral, a dear friend offered to be eight-year-old Deborah's minder and support. Deb was with us most of the time, but our friend kept an eye on her all the time and was ready to move in and take her off for a walk if it all became too much for her.

Getting over it

As adults, talking things through helps us make sense of things. Once we have told the story enough times, we have usually expressed our feelings, integrated the information into our lives and dealt with most of the trauma. Don't be surprised that your children ask the same questions over and over again or ask you to tell them the story about 'how Grandpa became sick and died' many, many times. It is their way of integrating the information and getting over the pain.

Telling the story — again and again and again

Children can also integrate difficult information through storybooks. One very nice way of helping a child deal with loss or trauma is to write them a small storybook about the event.

As in all good storybooks, it should begin with 'Once upon a time, a beautiful little baby boy/girl was born called . . . He/she lived with . . . (show your child's family members) at . . . (show your child's address)'. Add other information that personalises the story and sets it in a happy frame. Add the names of people and pets important in your child's life and how he/she is loved by and loves them.

'Then one day, a dreadful thing happened . . .' This is your opportunity to put what happened into age-appropriate language. Particularly when the sad event happened very rapidly, this gives your child a chance to catch up with the information he may not have been able to get immediately and to go over and over it until it is fully understood.

Describe the sadness and how people felt and then add lots of important memories — happy, funny and sad — so that your child can anchor them and enjoy them.

Finish the story with a positive message about how the beloved person or pet may no longer be physically in their lives but will always live on in their memories. 'Now, any time . . . (your child's name) is missing grandparent/pet, all he has to do is think about some of the lovely things that they did together.'

THE END

Post-script
Our children may want to read or have read the storybook every evening, every time someone comes over and may wish to take it to kindergarten or school to tell their whole class. Eventually, the trauma will be over and the book will lie neglected. Your job is done.

— Littlies

Don't go, Mummy

WE'VE ALL HAD THAT heart-rending experience. We need to leave. Our child doesn't want us to leave. We explain all the benefits of their staying. We elaborate on all the wonderful opportunities there will be once we are out of sight. We are convinced! They are not!

We peel them off like an octopus. We make a dash for the door. We depart to the sound of piercing wails. Long after we have driven away we can still hear them echoing in our ears.

We fret and worry till pick-up time, imagining our precious child upset and suffering.

'How did it go?' we tentatively ask.

'Oh! He was just fine. The moment you were out of sight, he settled down and had a wonderful time.'

The next time, our child starts as dawn is breaking.

'Mummy, am I going to kindy today?'

'Yes darling. You will have such a wonderful time there with so many wonderful things to do.'

'Mummy, I don't want to go. Please don't make me go.'

Some do, some don't
All babies are designed to be attached to their mother, to seek her out and to feel comforted and safe when they are in her arms. Surrounded by many other people fairly constantly in their lives, they learn that

they can trust other people to look after them.

Some babies are of the 'go to anyone' variety and others object if you make eye contact with them before they have had a chance to 'suss you out'.

As parents we are very tough on ourselves. We somehow believe that it is a mark of parental competence to have children who can part easily from us and manage well without us. Conversely, if we have a child who finds it hard to let us go, we somehow feel as if we have failed a parenting test. I think we are far too tough on ourselves.

The reality is that some children find it easy to be self-reliant and easily say goodbye and enjoy a new experience without us. Other children find this much more difficult. It is more a matter of our child's style and temperament than of upbringing.

Provided we do it at our child's pace, all children can learn that people other than their immediate family can be trusted to care for them.

Think of a daisy
It helps to think of ourselves as the centre of our child's world, rather like the centre of a daisy with ever-increasing petal sizes.

When our baby first begins to crawl they will go a few feet away from us, get busy for a while and then scuttle back when they feel the need for security or comfort. Soon, they feel able to go into the next room, but when it gets scary, they rush back to find us.

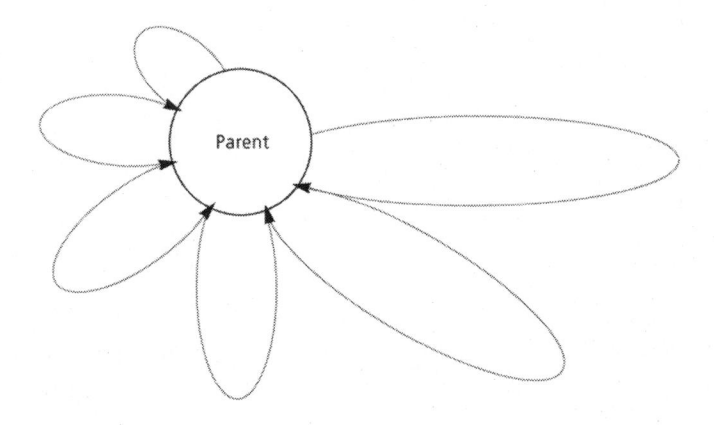

As they get older they are able to manage without us for increasingly longer intervals as they go to daycare, kindergarten, primary school, high school and eventually overseas.

Managing without us

What makes our children able to manage without us is three-fold.

First, it is their ability to hold us in their hearts and minds, so that they know we will return.

Second, their experience teaches them that we can go away and be sure to return within an interval of time that our child can manage.

Third, we replace ourselves with another trusted adult in the centre of the daisy. Dad, grandparents, aunties and uncles, babysitters, crèche caregivers and kindergarten teachers can all become people our child can trust to keep them safe, understand their wants and meet their needs.

Leaving easily

For most children, we go through a simple routine when we drop them at kindergarten. We walk in with them, we greet their teacher and they participate in hanging up their jacket and bag. We help them find their first activity.

When they are well settled in, we say goodbye and leave. They may look up and farewell us or they may be so engrossed in whatever they are doing that they barely notice or deign to farewell us.

We go off happy and secure in the knowledge that our child can manage without us.

But my child gets really upset

Some children interpret our behaviour completely differently. We walk in with them clinging and wailing, they refuse to look at the teacher — let alone greet them. They passively let us hang up their bag and jacket. They refuse to settle to any activity and reject our suggestions for what might be interesting.

What is going on here? These children interpret our intentions completely differently. The dialogue going on in their head is something like, 'So if I settle down to play, Mum will leave. So I can't possibly settle down to play, because that will make Mum leave.'

In trying to settle them in, we place them in an impossible conflict with themselves — and us!

Do something different

These children require a different approach. We take them in, we hang up their gear and, at this moment, there is no point in prolonging their agony. Ask your child, 'Who would you like to cuddle you while Mummy leaves?' Your child will always know who is their best 'centre of the daisy'.

Say to the caregiver, 'Can Jamie be with you while I go?' If necessary, peel him off, hand him over, kiss him goodbye and leave swiftly without a backward glance.

He may still be dreadfully upset

Your child may still be dreadfully upset. You may still have to depart with his cries ringing in your ears. But you have left him safely in someone's arms.

That person will comfort him and settle him into an activity. The main difference is that he knows the caregiver is there for the whole day and that he can rush to her any time he needs care or comfort. He will rapidly settle and be ready to join in the fun.

You can be like everyone else

Soon you will be like the rest of us. Your child will race away from you at the gate, scarcely remembering to say 'goodbye'. When you arrive to pick him up, he may even scream, 'Go away! I'm busy. I don't want to come home.'

Then you can be like the rest of us who cringe with embarrassment when we ponder what sort of home it is we run that our children don't even wish to return!

— *Littlies*

Managing tantrums

WHENEVER I AM IN a supermarket and see an angry or despairing child plaster themselves onto the floor and begin wailing and screaming, I immediately think 'Oh you poor little thing. Who on earth is ever going to come to your rescue?'

The 'poor little thing' I am fretting about is the parent! We've all had that awful moment when our child goes ballistically out of control and we have that nagging feeling that a 'good' parent would be able to prevent the tantrum in the first place.

The reality is that no one can continuously prevent a child from getting terribly upset or angry. However, sometimes when we sense that our child is winding up, we can do things that will head-off the major wobbly. Other times, there is nothing that we can do but weather it.

All tantrums are not created equal. If we can recognise what sort of tantrum it is, we can be effective in helping out children deal with the angry or despairing feelings that overwhelm them — and threaten to overwhelm us.

Tantrums of despair
Sometimes our children are dreadfully upset. The square peg won't go into the round hole, they expected to go and play in the park and now it is raining, Mum said 'No' to a third chocolate biscuit, their

friend just doesn't want to play with them, they just knocked their shin on the corner of the chair. Our child may be tearful, angry or both.

First, let's talk about the things that don't work well. Logical and reasoned explanations are of little help when our child is 'all feelings and no thinking'. Trying to calm them down and suggesting it is not worth so much fuss is not helpful when our child is revving up to full volume. Distraction may sometimes work but is usually very hard work for the parent.

What our children need is for us to say something that shows them we understand how upset they are. It is comforting to our child to have us put into words what they are feeling. If we are to be really convincing we need to use our tone of voice to match the intensity of their feelings.

'That puzzle just won't go right.'

'You are so disappointed that it is raining and we can't go to the park.'

'You really, really wanted another biscuit but it is too close to dinner.'

'You are so upset that your friend doesn't want to play right now.'

'Oooh! Your shin really, really hurts.'

Having said this, there is little else to add to the subject.

Now is the time to offer, 'Are you a big boy who needs a cuddle?' or the time-honoured magic approach 'Can Mummy kiss it better?' Just keep your arms around your child, don't say anything other than a few soothing sounds and wait. Pretty soon your child will have got over it and be ready for the next adventure.

Tantrums of control

Sometimes our strong-willed children will use a tantrum of anger to try to force us to change our mind. They are more likely to scream rather than cry. They may squirm and wriggle to get away while being changed. If they cannot get their own way through shouting or running, they may resort to hitting, shoving, spitting or yelling unkind or unacceptable words.

At this point, we often resort to threats of punishment if the behaviour continues. The problem with this approach is that it needs our child to be in a calm, thinking state to be able to understand the consequences of where his behaviour might be leading him and a yelling child is rarely able to hear us above his own noise.

We need to respond to a tantrum of control with distance rather than empathy. It may be easiest to walk away or it may be necessary to scoop our child up and pop him in a separate room.

Either way, there is little point in arguing or reasoning. Our child is too enraged to listen to what we have to say. It is much more effective to forget about negotiating and to pop our child in a quiet space to calm down.

Despair or control?

How can we tell if we are dealing with a tantrum of despair or a tantrum of control? The simplest way is to check our own feelings. If our first thought is 'You poor little thing,' then the odds are that it is a tantrum of despair and our child needs our support.

If our initial response is one of anger, if we feel pushed around by our small 'monster', then the odds are high that it is a tantrum of control and we are better off distancing ourselves from our child till they are ready to concede control and see it our way.

Still not sure?

If you are still not sure, try empathy first. 'Are you a big boy who needs a cuddle?' If it is a tantrum of despair, your child will come into your arms for some comfort.

If it is a tantrum of control, he is more likely to yell, 'Go away! I don't like you!'

This is the signal to create some distance between you — either by your going away or by scooping him into his room.

Many children, after a few minutes on their own, will switch from anger to upset and it is appropriate for us to match their feelings by offering them a cuddle if they are now ready for one.

Too-much day

The third type of tantrum often occurs when our child is overtired, over stimulated — or both. These often come after a perfectly lovely outing or party when our child has had an excellent time. They have been charming and delightful and everyone has told us how gorgeous they are.

We leave the situation and suddenly they turn into a hideous whirling dervish of flailing arms and legs and temper. What went wrong? How could they behave so badly when we have been to considerable effort to give them such a good time.

It took me a long time to understand that having a lovely time can also be very exhausting for our children and when their tiredness catches up they simply 'lose the plot'.

In these situations there is no magic answer. Often we just have to get through the situation as best we can. A nice calming bath, a quiet story time, a good night's sleep and our child will wake up ready to be their usual charming selves. They are likely to behave as if nothing happened. We may still be shattered!

— Littlies

Fun and games

A FEW WEEKENDS AGO, I had the chance to go away, just me and my ten-year-old daughter, for two whole days. We went to a tiny bach at Waiwera and spent the time just being together.

We played Canasta ferociously. I hadn't played since my teenage years and, other than chess, it is the only game I remember my late parents playing. My daughter is better at this game than I am. She is a better tactician and reads my 'poker-face' (excuse the mix of games here) as if my cards were transparent. She delighted in my weeping and wailing, and I delighted in her skill, memory and tactics.

We found a storm water drain that trickled warm water over the sand as far as the sea. We spent at least two solid hours creating rivers and moats, dams and islands. We yelled frantic instructions at each other. 'Dig here.' 'Make a pile here.' 'Faster, faster, it's all being swept away.' We didn't ponder where the water had come from, but we did wash our hands somewhat thoroughly afterwards!

We threw and caught tennis balls and frisbees. We bounced on a trampoline.

We walked together and admired the sunset and the sparrows and the trees and the shells.

We lit candles and meditated. Sometimes — and I consider this a major achievement from two noisy, gregarious, fun-loving people — we managed a silence of ten minutes.

We farewelled our holiday with an adventure playground visit and a three flavoured ice-cream.

As we drove back to Auckland, and to our usually hectic lives, my daughter said 'Thanks Mum, that is the best holiday we've ever had.'

It was a lovely compliment. Yet, I felt sad and remorseful. It was such a simple break and yet, in the raising of three children, I could not remember another time of such peace and enchantment. I regretted the number of times I had been too busy to laugh and play with my children.

I would like to think I learned something and that I will make changes.

— Parenting With Confidence

Making sure that fun really *is* fun for everyone

MOST OF US SUBSCRIBE to the idea that fun is good for us and good for our children. Fun is one important way of having quality time with our children.

There are three major purposes of having fun with our children.

- **The spiritual 'buzz' we get when people are having a good time together.** Most of us have had that wonderful experience of looking at our children, or our spouse and children, or a grandparent and grandchild, having noisy fun or a special quiet moment together. We've caught another adult's eye and a flood of gratitude and delight has passed between us. A truly magic moment. Let's have more of them.
- **Games are a great way of teaching children all sorts of skills** like ball-handling, racquet skills, general knowledge, counting, memory improvement and spelling.
- **Games are a great way of teaching qualities** like sportsmanship, gracious winning and gracious losing, courage, honesty, supportiveness to younger or less able people, taking turns and fairness.

Then how come, what starts off as a good idea and lots of fun, often finishes with shouting and tears?

The most important thing for us to remember is that, although it is wonderful for the Child in us to play and laugh and have a good time, someone has to remain the Adult. Too often, we become competitive and want to win at the cost of our child's self-esteem. Too often, we want to keep playing much longer than our child's endurance can manage. Too often, particularly if we are a Dad who is grabbing twenty minutes time with our child at the end of a busy working day, we forget that our child is tired and needs gentle cuddles and quiet stories, rather than chasing and wrestling.

Here are some ideas for making sure that fun *stays* fun:

Modify the game so that everyone, regardless of age or competence, feels equally successful. For instance, if you are throwing a ball to several children, make sure that throw is able to be caught by the recipient. If you are play fighting, only fight as hard as the child you are playing with can manage.

Stay in charge. It's your job to make sure that no one gets hurt. It's your job to see everyone plays fair and has fun. If you are dealing with a large age or ability-range, it is your job to see no one feels left out. If several children want to wrestle you at once, you may need to line them up and get them to take turns. Appoint the others as cheerleaders.

Unacceptable behaviour is unacceptable. All your normal household rules apply. No hitting, no hurting, no unkindness, no verbal abuse. Avoid being so keen to have fun that you allow unacceptable behaviour.

Don't send them out of the game 'forever'. It is inevitable that one of the children will not be able to cope. Avoid sending them away with a message that they are a 'wimp and a bad sport'. Call a five-minute break. Give the child some breathing space and/or a cuddle. Let them join in again, watch the others or go and do something else. Leave the opportunity for them to join you when they are ready.

Finish while everyone is having fun. It requires amazing judgement to finish on a pleasant note instead of when everyone is screaming and crying. When you see that trouble is brewing, finish the game and go and celebrate with afternoon tea.

Calm them down. Make it your job to return them to a pleasant and co-operative state.

Above all, enjoy your children and enjoy yourself.

— *Parenting With Confidence*

Shy children

First, we protect
There is something very endearing about shy children. They appear vulnerable and we move to protect them. In a world of loud, boisterous children who take off in car parks when we least expect it, it is a relief to have one who will stay near us, hold our hand and speak softly.

Next, we worry
And then, somehow, we find ourselves becoming worried. If they cannot even say 'Hello' to their teacher, how on earth are they going to be able to manage to find a group of children to join in with and play? If they cannot meet their beloved grandma's eye and say 'Lovely to see you, Grandma,' what about the less familiar adults whom they encounter and what about their peers?

We notice that adults begin by being very caring and patient. They crouch down to our child's level and try hard to engage them. They try every guaranteed child-conversation-opener they know. However, if it isn't working, we also notice that they give up and move away to another child who will appreciate their efforts more.

Finally, we become exasperated
It is awkward to have visiting parents say to their children, 'I'm sure

Jo will be out soon.' It is embarrassing to have your child be able to grab the gift but not able to say 'Thank you'. It is inappropriate to have your children march past their smiling, greeting teacher.

When we are starting to get that 'Here we go again' feeling, it may be that our child may not be just shy. They are likely to be tipping into rudeness.

Selective shyness

Sometimes we notice that our children are getting selective in their ability to meet, greet and farewell. Some days, they race out to say 'hello' to family members, sometimes they will only come out when they are ready or the present looks interesting. They are able to take the gift but not able to say 'Thank you' and we are starting to get fed up with saying, 'Please excuse her, she's shy, you know.'

And then, we remember or someone reminds us about how awful it was to be shy and maybe they will grow out of it or maybe 'That's just the way they are' and we start to feel unreasonable for having got irritated.

Kind people help keep them shy

When we try to insist that they say 'Hello' or 'Thank you' or 'I'd like the orange one, please', kind people — just as we are trying to hold firm — say 'Oh, don't worry, I understand.'

It is best if you can cue Grandma or the teacher beforehand. Enlist their help. Tell them that you are trying to teach your child to be courteous and you need their help. When they greet your child, could they please wait until they get a response and not excuse the child. The adults are a team who are supposed to be helping a child with appropriate behaviour.

So what is OK?

I think that a certain amount of natural reserve is attractive. Many people hold back a little till they find out if you are going to treat them well or badly. Many people are great listeners and do not need to give you every piece of information about themselves before you even had time to phrase an enquiry.

However, there does come a point where reserve tips into rudeness. It is simple courtesy to greet people when they greet you, to answer reasonable questions, to thank someone for a gift or a service or for inviting you.

Unless a child is normally unable to utter words, it is reasonable to expect them to be able to say, 'Nice to see you', 'Thank you for the ride', 'Thank you for a lovely party', in a normal voice, at an appropriate time, with a reasonable degree of enthusiasm and sincerity. Where children are capable of civilised interaction when it suits them, it would be hard not to come to the conclusion that, in matters of courtesy, they have shifted from 'I can't' to 'I won't'.

Supportive strategies

My first move would always be to give your child support and time to be able to say what needs to be said. Before you arrive, remind them about how pleased Grandma would be to be greeted nicely.

When you get to the door, put a supportive arm around their shoulders or hold their hand and prompt their behaviour. Say to them, 'Darling, say "*Hello, Grandma. Nice to see you.*" '

Wait. Keep your supportive arm there, but don't rush in to rescue your child. Your child has a minor tension to overcome. He or she has to struggle between *I don't want to do that because I find it hard* and *It is necessary for me to say a few appropriate words, nicely.* Sorting out the struggle in your child's mind may take a few seconds, which may feel like half-an-hour. Stand patiently and wait. Let your child solve the problem. It is your child's problem to solve.

If you are *this* clear about your expectations and *this* generous in your support and your child is still tearful or has a tantrum, the odds are very high that you are being challenged by a child who is both sensitive and strong willed. It is time to take action.

Calm action counts

Say, 'I need you to say 'Hello, Grandma' and we are not going in until you are ready to do that.' (If it is at home, quietly insist that he stays in his room until he is ready to greet Grandma politely.)

If your child declines to get out, wait quietly with him in the car.

'That's OK. We'll wait till you are ready.' If your child declines at the door, take him back to the car and wait quietly. You are showing your child that ordinary courtesy is not negotiable and, as long as you don't make it exciting by persuading, threatening or punishing, but show you are quietly determined that your instruction will be followed, your child will be ready quite soon.

If you are teaching your child to greet his kindergarten teacher, I somewhat facetiously recommend taking a thermos of coffee and a book to read in the car. You may never get to drink your coffee, but your child will understand that you mean what you say, you are prepared to wait it out and nothing much more will happen until he is ready to greet politely.

Occasionally, I have known a really determined child to hold out for a kindy morning. Invariably, they have been ready the next time they go to kindergarten.

It is a battle worth winning, for your child's sake.

Remember why it is worth the struggle

If this seems too harsh, remember that courtesy is a behaviour and a habit that can be learned. People who are reasonably outgoing and genuinely polite tend to have much easier and more pleasant interactions with others and are better liked. People respond well to friendly, courteous behaviour and tend to give up on boorish behaviour.

Protect your child's natural reserve, support them to overcome shyness and insist that they 'meet and greet' politely and graciously.

— Parenting With Confidence

Getting our children to do as they are told

Why bother?
When we ask a child to do something, it is a good idea to remember that this has a short-term, medium-term and long-term objective.

The *short-term* is because we need to carry out some simple and often-repeated task.

- Let's get you dressed, please
- I'll do up your seat-belt, please
- Go and get your homework, please
- Pack your bag for tomorrow, please.

If our child just does what we have asked them to as soon as possible, it saves a lot of nagging, whining and arguing, on both sides, and our child is learning a useful skill.

What about the *medium-term*? How many requests do you think you will make to your child before he leaves home? What if every request meets with the same opposition as it does to 'Put your socks on now'? So another reason to get your child to do as he is told now is to save yourself some sanity for the future.

And *long-term*? When a child is persistently non-compliant, they may sabotage their relationship with their parents and family, they may sabotage their learning opportunities, they may have fewer and fewer friends. The same self-restraint needed to be reasonably compliant serves us well in the ordinary frustrations of learning new skills and being good friends.

Being good is good for kids
Hal Urban in his book *20 Things I Want My Kids To Know* says that as human beings we *need* to be good. There is a relationship between old-fashioned goodness, health and well-being.

I often work with parents to help them get their children to do as they're told. When I follow up a week or so later I often have a somewhat puzzled parent saying to me. 'I don't quite understand. We have been so much tougher on him and he seems so much happier.'

It's true. Our children feel happier when they are doing what is expected of them. It feels right to them and they feel more comfortable when they are getting it right.

Asking
It all starts when we ASK our child to do something.

Sometimes, it is just this simple. We ask our child to do something and they do it. This is a good time for showing appreciation. 'Thank you. That was a great help,' is a lovely way to let your child know that you value their effort.

If it's not a 'Yes', it's a 'No'
Sometimes you will get instant compliance but, often, you will be dealing with non-compliance. To a simple request such as 'Take those cups out, please', non-compliance comes in various guises.

- It's not my turn
- Why do you always ask me?
- It's too hard
- I don't want to
- Will you help me?
- I'll just finish the 500-piece puzzle
- Those aren't my cups.

Or there are the non-verbal responses:

- Moan
- Grizzle
- Shrug Mum out of the way
- Laugh at her
- Ignore.

The Three Cons

Barbara Coloroso, in her book, *Kids Are Worth It*, talks about 'the three cons' that children will come up with when asked to do something that they do not wish to do.

First, there is the *angry* response. 'It's not fair. It's not my turn. I'm not going to. You can't make me. You're not the boss of me.'

These are the sorts of children where we wind up thinking 'It's much simpler to do it myself.' If you do it yourself, the down side is your child misses out on essential skills and you are teaching them that intimidation works.

Second, there is the *sad* response. These are always delivered in a pathetic whine. 'It's not fair. You always ask me. I did it yesterday. It's too hard. Why do you always ask me?' These children are the masters of guilt induction.

The third style of con is harder to pick up. It involves *distancing*. Your child goes deaf, turns to do something else, looks at you blankly as if you just asked something incomprehensible or laughs and runs away. This leaves us feeling disempowered.

Telling is better than yelling

It is no use calling out from a distance. *ASK* once, from wherever you are. Wait ten seconds. By now you know if the answer is *YES* or *NO*.

If the answer is *NO*, you need to move from *ASK* to *TELL*. Move right next to where your child is, stand tall and say firmly, 'I'd like you to take those cups out, now' and wait for ten seconds.

You don't need to shout, you don't need to reason, you don't need to persuade. You have just given your child a very powerful message that you intend him to do as you have asked. Just this action — going close, asking powerfully and waiting — will get you compliance about 80% of the time.

First, you are not calling from a distance. The fact that you have taken the trouble to go over means that your child knows that you're serious.

Second, you should use a quiet voice. When you yell at your child, you are showing him that *you* are out of control. When you use a quiet voice, you are demonstrating that you are in control of *you*, so you are far more convincing as the person in control of him.

From NO to NO WAY

Some children just don't believe you. They may be very strong-willed or their experience up till now may be that if they put up enough argument, fuss or distance, they don't have to do as they are asked.

If you have ASKED, waited ten seconds, moved to TELL powerfully, and waited ten seconds, you will know for sure whether your child intends to do as you have asked — or not.

If he is going to comply, he will be doing as you asked. Any other action, means he has graduated from NO to NO WAY.

Escalating behaviour

According to the way he demonstrated NO — mad, sad or distancing — you can expect that he will escalate that behaviour.

If his initial response was anger, he will escalate to greater anger. He may shout or push you out of the way.

If his initial response was sadness, he will escalate to distress. He may be so overcome with grief that he collapses in hysterical sobs.

If his initial response was to ignore you, he will turn away from you, move away from you, not in the direction of the cups, or even run away.

Your child has moved from NO to NO WAY.

Hand the problem over

Now it is time for us to think 'I've asked you to do something. Nothing else — in the way of goods or services from me — is going to happen until that is done.' The most powerful action to show our child we mean what we say is to put emotional distance between ourselves and our child. This way we hand the problem over to our child and our child has to wrestle with the problem. They have to contend with the tension between 'I don't want to do it' and 'It looks like I'll have to.'

Give them space to think
With a toddler, the 'scoop and dump' approach is the most effective. Scoop them up, pop them into their room or cot and walk out briefly. Go back in and ask 'Are you ready?' If they come into your arms for a cuddle, the odds are that they are ready to comply. If they shout at you, they are not ready and you will need to come back again in a little while.

With preschool or primary-aged children, send or take them to their room and tell them they can come out when they are ready to do as you have asked.

With an older child, or a younger one who is hard to get to go to their room, you distance from them. Go elsewhere, get busy, remember what you asked for. If your child approaches you for information or services, say pleasantly, 'Certainly. As soon as you have done … (whatever it was you requested)… I'd be happy to think about that' and leave the problem with your child.

How long will it take?
I have no idea. The important thing for you to be thinking is 'I have asked you to do something. Nothing else is going to happen in your world until that is done.' The important thing is that your child learns, through experience, that once a parent has made a request, nothing else is happening until it is done.

But what if I am in a hurry?
This is not some magic trick that will force a non-compliant child to change their mind. This is a way to show your child that, when a parent asks them to do something the expectation is that they will do it and that nothing much else will happen until it is done.

When you are going out in five minutes, it is not the best time to begin compliance training.

Where do I start?

There are two good opportunities every day.

First thing in the morning insist that the first thing you ask for is done. Your child might need to wait in their room for some time until they have worked out who is boss for the day but, unless that boss is you, the day is not going to get any better.

Do the same with the second and the third request. By the time your child has been compliant three times, they are on-track to being compliant for the rest of the morning.

The other good time is when you pick up your child after school. Start with not allowing your child into the house till she is capable of carrying in her own gear. Next insist that your child puts her lunchbox on the sink and her homework in the homework spot.

Once you have established yourself as the boss for the afternoon, the rest of the day should go much more smoothly.

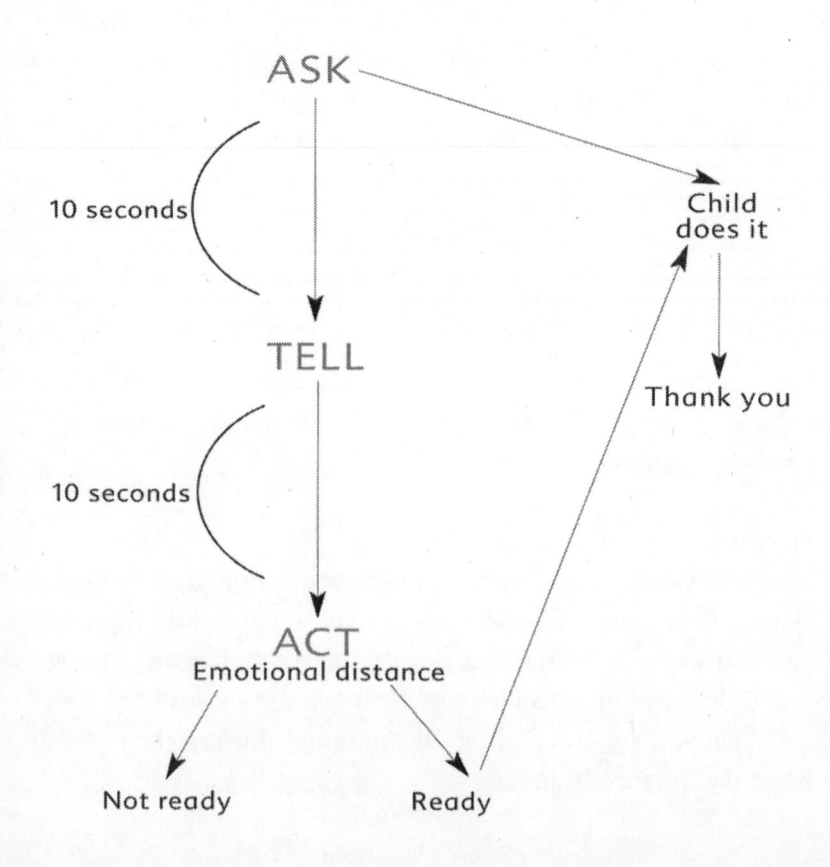

```
                    ASK
                   /   \
        10 seconds(     \
                   \     \
                    v     >  Child
                   TELL      does it
                   /   \       ^  |
        10 seconds(     \      |  v
                   \     \     | Thank you
                    v     \    |
                    ACT    \   |
            Emotional distance |
                   /    \      |
                  v      v-----+
              Not ready  Ready
```

Compliance is a habit

We need to change our child's thinking, in response to a parental request, from 'Maybe I will and maybe I won't' to 'I may not want to do that, but it looks like I have to.'

If our children are doing more-or-less what we ask them, most of the time, both our lives and their lives become much simpler and we can both enjoy each other's company more. Our children become pleasant to be with and we will choose to spend more time with them.

So that we can enjoy each other's company is the best reason I know for developing our children's compliance habit.

— *Parenting With Confidence*

When your child is being bullied

THE CALL OFTEN COMES in this form:

'My child is dreadfully unhappy. He used to be such a bright-eyed, bushy-tailed little chap, full of confidence — and now he has changed. His self-esteem seems so low and he doesn't want to go places. He is starting to have tummy aches in the morning and he just doesn't seem to know what is wrong.'

When did it change? Often there was a pivotal time, which may be immediate or gradual, but the child has felt increasingly picked on by someone.

Bullying continues to be a dreadful problem for many children. Many of us have been taught from our childhood to tough things out, not to complain and above all not to 'tell tales'.

- 'Just walk away.'
- 'Don't show them you are afraid.'
- 'Find someone else to play with.'
- 'Give as good as you get!'

So if this advice is not helping, what can a parent do?

Listen with empathy
When he tells you about something that was unpleasant for him, reflect his feelings and respond with a similar intensity:

- 'How awful for you.'
- 'What a nasty thing to do.'
- 'That is just a dreadful thing to have happen to you.'
- 'How unkind.'

Focussed empathy may be all you need
Show your child you are listening and want the information.

'So here's the plan. Every afternoon after school, I am going to ask you how your day was and I'm going to take notes because what you say is important to me.' Then do that for a fortnight. Each day, listen with empathy, write notes, don't problem solve.

Often, by the sixth day, your child may not have anything bad to report, they are the best of friends and the careful listening that you have done enables the child to solve the problem herself.

And if it is not enough?
If focussed listening doesn't solve the problem, you know that it is too hard for your child to solve on his own and adult intervention is going to be needed.

Remember that bullying is bad for your child and bad for the bully. You are well justified in seeking help.

Start with the classroom teacher
If you get the 'Well, we can't be watching them all the time' treatment, stick with the important facts:

- My child is unhappy.
- Someone is being unkind to her.
- I need your help.

Remember, that a teacher's role is to be responsible for your child's safety *in loco parentis* (in the place of the parent) and the school has an obligation by law to watch out for your child's safety.

Be prepared to go higher up
If speaking with the teacher is not effective, make an appointment to

see the Principal and if that is not effective contact the Chairman of the Board of Trustees.

Once may not be enough
The teacher may intervene and it may all work for several weeks, but then it starts up again. Go back to the school and find the person who was the most helpful to you.

Start with 'Last time you were able to work such wonders for my child, we need your magic touch again.'

And what if the bully is a teacher?
This does not happen often but, when it does, **it is very damaging for the child involved.**

The majority of teachers are wonderful, caring people who treat our children as if they were their own and in whom we can have great confidence. However, there is the occasional exception. There are very few of us who cannot remember a teacher who made our lives miserable. The misery that is heaped upon children by a cruel, bullying teacher is great and may result in a child who is tearful, frightened, reluctant to go to school and unable to learn there.

Sometimes our children are direct targets. The teachers may single them out, denigrate their work or their ideas in front of peers, mete out unreasonable punishments or pick on them with sarcastic, humiliating comments.

Sometimes our children are indirect targets. These are the good and diligent children who do not put a foot wrong but find themselves continuously in a state of anxiety in case they inadvertently incur the wrath of this teacher and wind up in the sort of trouble they see their peers experience.

Often the same teacher has very good relationships with colleagues and parents and it is very hard to believe (both for parents and principals) that this person is a bully in the classroom or playground.

Listen to what is being said about the teacher
If her reputation is 'firm but fair', it is unlikely that she is bullying. If the words:

- Sarcastic
- Picks on some children or
- Has favourites

are her reputation, you are dealing with a bully.

Follow the same steps as with any other bully

- Listen to your child.
- Gather information.
- Go higher up.
- Stick to the point:
    My child is dreadfully unhappy; I need your help.
- Once may not be enough.

Final comment

Bullying is a serious problem and we need to protect our children from this form of abuse. Some bullying is obvious and some bullying is subtle and hard to prove. Dealing with it is one of the very difficult but essential parts of parenting.

— Parenting With Confidence

Oh no! Mum's on another health kick!

Formula for disaster

It all starts innocently enough. We decide that the family is going to eat healthy. We call a family meeting and explain to our children how much we love them and care for their well-being. We declare, 'From tomorrow, we are all going to be eating healthy foods.' We cheerfully explain all the benefits to our family and they are delighted that veges are in, chocolate is out and they thank us for our care and consideration.

'Yeah! Right!' as my children say when mustering maximum sarcasm.

Formula for success

There is a much easier way to get your family's co-operation when you change the household over to healthy eating. *Never let them know that this is happening.* The moment they know you are planning to eliminate the unhealthy food that they love, they will regard all healthy food with enormous suspicion. Their resistance will be up and they will be on the alert, ready to yell 'Oooh, yuck!' at anything that even resembles healthy food.

So, how do you change to healthy eating without letting them know that it is happening?

- Reduce
- Replace
- Run out

These three simple steps are your formula for developing healthy eating habits without the family being any the wiser!

Begin with the end in mind

Steven Covey, a management guru, talks about 'beginning with the end in mind'. If it is good enough for adult managers, it is worth thinking about for your family.

Right now you may be eating pre-sliced-white bread. Eventually you would like everyone to eat rye bread. Start by changing to light-brown, fine-textured, pre-sliced bread. Once that has been accepted, get slightly darker bread, and before you know it, they'll be eating rye bread with pumpkin seeds!

Present 'new food' without comment. Avoid guaranteed-to-raise-resistance comments like, 'This is absolutely yummy.' They only invite 'gross!' as a response.

If you want your children to eat veges, they are more likely to if they (the veges — not the children!) come peeled, raw and accompanied by a dip.

If your child's ideal dip has mayonnaise made with sweetened condensed milk, begin by changing to an all-oil mayonnaise that at least looks thick and creamy. Once that has been accepted, change to the 'lite' version. After that, you may find that they can cope with yoghurt-based dips and mayos.

Keep old containers

Try low cunning. Keep the old jar that contained the unhealthy version and tip in the healthier version. The trick is to keep your family from being forced to confront a diet change so they do not go into resistance mode.

Once they have accepted the new version, don't give the game plan away. It is tempting to say, 'See! It is the healthy version and you didn't even know that you were eating it,' but you have just guaranteed that every food in the household will now be sharply scrutinised for any sign of healthiness and then promptly rejected.

Run out of things
Begin by quietly letting your supplies of unhealthy food run down. When someone bleats, 'Where's the sugar-coated cereal?' don't launch into a lecture about how bad it was and how you have replaced it with something that is high-fibre, nutritious, has the heart-tick and that they should be grateful to have such a caring and loving mother.

Mutter vaguely and apologetically, 'There doesn't seem to be any in the cupboard.' Go and look behind a few things (even though you know that it isn't there). If absolutely pushed, you can even declare that you will try to remember to get some next time you go shopping. Just don't try hard enough.

Am I being deceitful? Maybe. It's just that I have found that when you make enthusiastic announcements of reform, the resistance goes up.

Have treat foods available
Your family will feel very hard done-by if you eliminate treat foods. Don't expect them to do without, just gradually change the type of food and/or the quantity.

I don't know about your household but, in mine, morning tea, afternoon tea and coffee-after-dinner all call for the inclusion of something different from the three main meals.

For morning and afternoon teas for children, by all means cut out lots of biscuits and chips. Put out one biscuit, a tiny packet of chips. Gradually, start substituting dried fruit, cheese cubes, nuts (large and unsalted).

The hardest one for me has always been chocolate. I alternate between overkill, no chocolate and 'one-piece-only'. It is better when there is none in the house, but the self-discipline — not to mention the taste — of 'one-piece-only' is much more satisfying.

Out of sight is out of mind

It is too hard for most of us to look at highly desirable, bad-for-us food and say, 'No!'

If there are foods that you don't want your family to eat, the simplest way is to not have them in the house.

If you feel you need them 'just in case', don't let them be seen as they enter the house or you will just encourage the small detectives on endless hunting missions.

Do everyone a favour and keep them well out of sight and well out of reach.

Your job — their job

You are not running a smorgasbord. Each meal, make available the foods that you think are appropriate and let your children be guided by their appetites as to how much of what is going they will eat.

Your job is — five times a day — to make available healthy food that your family more-or-less likes. Their job is to decide what they will do with that opportunity.

Good health and good luck!

— Fitness Life – Kids' Life

Supporting children when they are upset

THIS WAS AN INTERVIEW with Diane Levy by the editor of *Essentially Food*.

Q: How do you approach your child if they do not want to tell you why they are upset or angry?

A: With extreme caution! And with respect!

If they don't want to talk about being upset, you have to ask yourself why your child does not want to talk to you. There are often several issues at stake for them.

1. Are they too angry or too upset to speak?

If you get the 'Go away!' response, a good way is to say to your child 'You seem really cross. If you'd like to talk about it, I'd like to hear about it. Come and find me when you are ready.'

That way, you give them a nice 'warm' space to sort themselves out and you may be able to approach them later, or they may be ready to approach you.

2. Is it a loyalty-to-someone-else issue? OR

3. Is it because the other times when they have told you about something, they didn't fancy the way you responded. Ask yourself 'when he/she tells me what is wrong, do I listen with empathy, am I critical, judgmental, sympathetic, quick to blame? Do I race to offer solutions — unasked for?'

We need to think how we can approach the problem next time. The way we listen to our children will actually encourage them to approach us another time — or not!

If you get the listening right most of the time — then when it's really bad, you would up the chances that you will be the one they come to.

Different age groups probably require different approaches

Q: How do you best help an upset 6 year old?
A: By asking 'Do you need a cuddle or do you need space?'. That actually creates a 'warm' place for the child to choose how they like to be comforted. If necessary, they can say, 'I need space' and go off without our getting 'huffy'. And that is being respectful of our children. It leaves them a choice whether to handle their feelings by themselves or whether to use parental support.

It leaves the door open for them to first go away, change their mind and come back to us for support.

Q: How do you best help an upset 15 year old?
A: Teenagers very often first want space and then they want to run the problem past a peer. Often, the parent is the last resort. The nicest way to approach them is with food in the space that they've gone off to. Arrive with a plate of afternoon tea. Say, 'You look awfully cross to me — whenever you're ready to talk about it, I'd love to hear what happened.' That leaves it open to them.

What about the more serious cases of upset

Q: Are there any tell-tale signs for parents if a child doesn't want to talk but seems unusually upset or angry?
A: Often, the worst way to start is to say 'What's wrong?' You can start by describing your worry. For example, 'You've seemed really upset and cross for a while now. I'm worried about you.'

If you are worried there is bad stuff going on, you may not necessarily get the best information directly from your child. For teenage kids, you must set up a really good network amongst their friends and the parents of their friends. You must take every opportunity to try to get to know them and their parents. Driving them places is a good idea. It gives you a legitimate excuse to get to know your children's friends and their parents. If you are seriously worried you then have a network of others that you can approach for help or information.

It helps to be vigilant and look out for other clues. For example, if the upset has been going on for a long time. Changes in eating patterns would worry me or a child not sleeping. Or if their social habits change a lot, like from being very gregarious to suddenly spending a lot of time at home, or the other way round.

You can also say to your child 'I'm worried about you, but it's OK if you don't want to talk to me. Is there anybody else that you would like to talk to?'

When your children are upset, you take every opportunity you can to find out how you can help them. There is a lovely concept in business circles: leader as servant. Ask them 'Is there anything at all that I can do to help?'

Q: There are sudden upsets and then there are predictable upsets, say a close relative is dying of cancer. How do you prepare your children? What do you tell them, how much do you tell them, and when do you tell them?
A: Children do best on information and they always sense when there is a secret. If the 'sad thing' going on is going to become public knowledge, then I think our children certainly need the information.

- Try and keep it age-suitable.
- Talk about what is going on. For example, 'you may have noticed that grandma is looking very tired lately' and then 'let's talk about it'.
- Pick your timing.
- Think: what is the child's level of discretion. If you want it to be a secret, you need to remember that a secret is quite burdensome to children. And you can only tell secrets to those that can hold them!

Younger children do better on a small chunk of information, followed by an invitation that they can ask as many questions as they like — now or whenever they want to. Very often they have nothing much to say at the time, but they may well wish to raise questions when they have digested the initial information.

Give them the opportunity to come back with questions. If you want your children to feel secure with something that's troubling them, leave them the opportunity to ask as many times as they need to. Remember that not everyone processes information by talking it through. There are some people — and children are people too! — who process information by thinking about it. This process may have no visible clues that anything is going on.

With little children you can expect that if something bad is going on, they will want the story many, many, many times. They are less likely to ask exploratory questions and more likely to want to hear the same story all over again. Older children are more likely to ask you exploratory questions.

Always leave an open door for them to come back with concerns or more questions.

Q: How do you cope as a parent in an upsetting situation that affects the whole family?
A: I think showing your children how sad or upset you are is perfectly appropriate. But if you are overwhelmed with sadness or grief or anger to the point of not being able to function, that is more than the children can handle.

My best example is my mother's funeral. My daughter was eight years old. A good friend said to me 'I'll be on hand — and she can always come to me.'

So this was like a 'Plan B' for me. If I can handle it — fine. And if I can't, then someone else can handle my daughter, so that I can deal with my own feelings. I was enormously grateful to my friend.

It is a positive thing to show your child your feelings, but if you are overwhelmed to the point of not being able to care for your child, then you have to make other arrangements.

Q: How much involvement should children really have in a funeral?
A: I think that is a personal and also a very cultural thing. Most of us have come from an era where children were totally shielded and were in fact excluded, while adults went away and dealt with life-crises like funerals.

Exclusion is very shocking to children. I think the more involvement the better, without giving them more responsibility than their age can handle. And only give them involvement that you will respect their opinion on. You have got to exercise your wisdom for what you ask their opinion for. For example, your child may suggest 'Cookie Monster' would be great as a picture on the headstone for aunty so-and-so. If you are not going to follow through on their opinion — don't ask them.

Q: Is it OK to cry in front of your children?
A: There is now a myth going around in our society that 'everybody has to cry' — but we have to be respectful of both adults and children and know that there are many ways to express your feelings.

We show the guidelines for our children as to what is appropriate behaviour. Particularly in a strange and unusual situation that the child hasn't been in before, they will look to us as a guide to appropriate behaviour.

Q: What support systems are available to upset children?
A: My preference is always for the parent to be the one that the child talks to. I want to see very early experiences that show our children that their parent is the one that they can come and talk to when they are angry or upset.

But adolescents sometimes don't want to talk to their parents. It is also very hard in a divorce situation to handle the child's worries about the other parent. A child may worry about 'who will look after Dad now' but may not be able to talk to Mum about it. Or, not surprisingly, Mum may find it an infuriatingly difficult question to answer nicely.

You can stick a little note under the door with names and addresses of people that are available for them to talk to. Suggest to adolescent children 'Have you thought about a school counsellor, or someone else in the family, or Youthline?' Offer that you will set it up for them if they like — because children sometimes find it hard to bridge the gap. That way you also give your child permission that you won't be hurt if they wish to speak to someone else. When it's too hard to speak to a child, notes are absolutely invaluable.

Q: In summary, what would you emphasise?
A: When your child is upset:

- Don't blame them.
- Don't criticise them.
- Don't lecture them.
- Don't offer solutions unless invited.

It is OK to say, 'I have some ideas. Would you like to hear them?' And then respect the answer!

— Essentially Food

Peaceful holidays

SCHOOL HOLIDAYS ARE A great opportunity.

Some of us face seven weeks of summer school holidays with dread. Our internal and public monologue goes something like 'How absolutely ghastly! Fifty days without relief. How on earth will I occupy them? I can't bear the thought of fifty days of fighting. Who was out to punish mothers when they thought up a long summer holiday?!'

Others of us look forward to the school and kindergarten holidays. 'Great!! No school lunches. No getting children ready in time for school. No time pressures. It's a lot of work but somehow the pressures seem less.'

And holidays can be a great opportunity to pay attention to some of the behaviours that we have been too tired and too stretched to deal with during term time. We can use the holidays to get our children's more antisocial behaviours in line so that they can start the new school year more class and playground-ready.

What do you do when your child hits other children and behaves aggressively?

The best way of stopping this behaviour is to be clear in your own mind that hitting (and while we are discussing this let's include biting, pushing, snatching, throwing and general unkindness) is an unacceptable and unjustifiable behaviour — even if 'she hit me first'.

Once we have that clear in our own minds, we are in a position to respond swiftly and surely to these behaviours.

For the purposes of this article, I am going to assume that the children are from the same family — ours. (We may not have permission to deal with other people's children.)

There are three ways we find out about hitting and each requires a different response.

You see one child hit another

Remove her to another room. As you are moving her, say — as quietly and calmly as you can manage — 'You know that you are not allowed to hit.' Then say, 'I'll be back in a couple of minutes to see if you are ready to join the family again.'

In taking this action right away, you are showing her that hitting is not part of acceptable behaviour in your household. If *she* wishes to rejoin the family, she will need to get *herself* into a different frame of mind. If she is finding the whole situation too difficult to deal with, you are giving her a calm space in which to take a break.

When you return ask her 'Are you ready to join the family?' You can tell by the way she answers if she has calmed down or if she needs more time. If she wants to stay there, just say 'You come out when you are ready' and she will join you again when she has had enough space and time.

If she hits again, even if it is five minutes later, do the same. This way, you are showing her, and anyone else (short!) witnessing, that hitting will not be tolerated in your home.

Someone comes crying to you

'She hit me.' Focus on the crying one. Put an arm around her and say 'How awful for you. Would a cuddle help?' If she accepts the cuddle from you, just hold still, don't add advice, mutter soothing noises and trust that she will reach a wise decision.

We do not know what that wise decision might be. Maybe she will decide not to annoy the 'hitter'. Maybe she will decide to get away faster the next time. Maybe she will decide to stay near the grown-ups for a while until the child who hit is feeling less dangerous.

Unless there is blood involved, don't go and growl at the hitting child. That puts the crying one in the position of telltale instead of aggrieved.

You hear things heating up
Get in early. If you wait for it to go away, it won't. The odds are very high that it will wind up with someone being hurt and then you will have to intervene anyway, so you might as well get up now!

It is important not to attribute blame. If you try to find out who started it, you will have to listen to the case for the prosecution, the case for the defence, all the counterclaims and you are unlikely to be any the wiser.

Much better to walk in and use a no-blame phrase and stop the war from breaking out. My favourite no-blame phrase is 'This isn't working.' It describes the situation well. It doesn't invite argument, though it is unlikely anyone waits for an invitation to argue!

You may like to use diversion like 'Let's all have afternoon tea.'

Alternatively, you may want to teach your children that you will not accept fighting. Follow up 'This isn't working' with 'You go to your room. And you go to your room. I'll set the timer.' Set the timer for ten minutes. At the end of ten minutes, call out 'Time's up. You can come out when you are ready,' and leave it to each child to decide when she is ready.

Once you have used this a few times, you can approach a potential battle scene with fairly heavy footsteps. You may be amazed to find out how often the protagonists will stop fighting, gang up on you and declare themselves to be 'friends'. Well, you did want them not to fight!

If you use this whenever you hear the temperature heating up between your children they will learn one of two things. Either they will learn not to fight *or* they will learn to fight very quietly. Either way, you have taught them a useful skill for home, classroom and playground.

Have a great holiday.

— *Essentially Food*

It's never too late to set up routines

Sow an act . . . reap a habit; sow a habit . . . reap a character; sow a character . . . reap a destiny

George Dana Boardman

I WATCHED IN AMAZEMENT as Anthony, aged nine, got up from the table and automatically took his plate, his cutlery and his glass to the kitchen sink. Why couldn't my children do that? It wasn't as if they didn't have the co-ordination. It wasn't as if they wouldn't do it, if reminded. They would even clear the *whole* table, if asked. What had impressed me was that Anthony did it automatically.

Maybe, just maybe, if I could get my child to put his lunchbox on the sink and hang up his school jumper, we might have a great destiny in the making. And even if his entire destiny isn't at stake, the preservation of my vocal cords and the lowering of my blood pressure would be goals worthy of consideration.

At the beginning of each school year, we often make unspoken resolutions. They tend to revolve around children getting changed after school or not making a fuss about homework or washing hands before meals — and I mean washing, not the rub soap and run the tap so Mum thinks there has been serious hand washing going on.

Is there a simple way of making life easier between three-thirty and bedtime? It is definitely not too late to kick-start some useful ways of making our parenting life simpler so that we do not have to battle to get through routines every day.

Here are some ideas that I have found useful in building my children's planning abilities so that they can develop good time-management strategies and become responsible for the implementation and completion of tasks.

You be the scribe — write in the 'fun stuff'
Collect pen and paper and afternoon tea and say to your child, 'I've got some ideas about how we could make your afternoon simpler.' Start to list what he needs to do between now and dinner-time.

> Afternoon tea
>
> 15-minute break
>
> 15-minute break
>
> 30-minute favourite TV programme

This will appear to be a fairly attractive set of options and by now you should have his full attention.

Help him own his responsibilities
Ask him, 'What are your homework responsibilities?' and add those in. Try and break them down into tasks that can be done in about ten to fifteen minute blocks. Then add the house-helping responsibilities.

Give him ownership and suitable power to choose
In helping you to construct the list, you give him ownership of the responsibilities. Now give him the power to choose the order in which he wishes to do things. Add a list of squares on the left-hand side and tell him that these are squares for him to write in the order.

We always worry that our children will choose all the fun stuff first and then moan and groan about the 'work' ones. I think we underestimate the intelligence of our children. Within a small number of days, you will find your child will be organising himself into a sensible alternating of work and play activities.

- ☐ Afternoon tea
- ☐ 15-minute break
- ☐ 15-minute break
- ☐ 30-minute favourite TV programme
- ☐ Learn 4x table
- ☐ Spelling list
- ☐ Write five sentences
- ☐ Reading
- ☐ Set the table
- ☐ Feed the dog

Give him recognition and power to choose the method

Lastly, put a set of squares on the right-hand side and tell him these are for ticking off the tasks as they are completed. Ask him whether he would like to call you and show you when each task is done or to show you when all are done. Some children need your support and recognition every step of the way. Being involved every ten minutes and being lavish in your admiration for what he has achieved is a small price to pay for diligence.

Other children like to do everything and then show it to you. Both ways are equally valid, but stay alert to the child who says, 'Everything's done, Mum, I'm just going next door to play.' Smile brightly and say, 'That's lovely darling. Now take me on an inspection tour.' You will be amazed how often this leads to 'Oh! Just wait a minute! I'll just . . .' and he vanishes to complete something or even several things.

This is definitely not magic. It will not turn a surly, unco-operative child into a helpful charmer. It is, however, useful for the child who is

☐ Afternoon tea	☐
☐ 15-minute break	☐
☐ 15-minute break	☐
☐ 30-minute favourite TV programme	☐
☐ Learn 4x table	☐
☐ Spelling list	☐
☐ Write five sentences	☐
☐ Reading	☐
☐ Set the table	☐
☐ Feed the dog	☐

moderately willing but keeps forgetting what he was there for in the first place. It is also useful for the child who has a lot on and has trouble ordering it in his head and it is definitely useful for the tired Mum who is getting fed-up with trying to keep three children on track at the same time.

This will work just as well to remind a child of the five steps he needs to be ready in the morning. If your child is just edging into reading, write the words and put a little picture next to it.

It is also a great one for all children who are excellent at forgetting. Pin a checklist near their bag with things that should be in their bag every day. Then you never have to remember what should be in it. All you have to do each day is say, 'Check the checklist' and follow up to make sure that they do.

Similarly, it will pay you once each term to make a 'Daily Special' checklist for the different items required on particular days. Remember to be specific. Writing, 'togs' may not mean 'and towel' to the child who is used to using Mum's memory and hasn't exercised his own.

Tuesday —
Swimming Togs
Towel
Comb
 Plastic Bag for wet things
Flute
Music
Notebook
Theory

It requires some work to set up, but it will save you lots of shouting, reprimanding and arguing.

And, who knows? You may even be setting up the habit of planning!

> *We are what we repeatedly do. Excellence, then,*
> *is not an act, but a habit.*
>
> Aristotle

— Essentially Food

Toddler-proofing your baby

IT DOESN'T SEEM SO long ago that Vernon and I had a serious discussion about family size. We couldn't possibly have a second child because we adored our first-born so much. It would simply be unfair to have another.

Luckily, our second child arrived sooner than expected and we discovered what all parents have to discover for themselves: love multiplies rather than needs to be divided.

However, if I were to do it all over again, I would focus less on the arrival of the newborn and more on the toddler, less on the feeling and more on the behaviour. And I would be much more honest.

Honest? Yes! Honest!

Don't overdo the sales pitch
I don't quite understand why, but we, who are normally very honest people, feel obliged to tell our young children amazing whoppers:

- We are having a baby and she is going to be your baby.
- It is going to be so lovely for you to have a baby to play with.
- She is going to be your friend.
- You are going to have to help look after her.

And our friends weigh in with:

- You are so lucky. You are going to be a big brother.

Within twenty-four hours after his sibling's birth, your toddler is likely to feel horribly betrayed.

No way is she *his* baby. *He* was only allowed to hold her briefly once and even then she only cries and doesn't even open her eyes. How does this compare with what he may do with all the other things that are his — like his truck and his teddy?

The baby cannot be played with, is a pretty useless friend at this stage and is not available for looking after. How lucky does this toddler feel?

We have lots of laws in our country about delivering what we have promised. Thank goodness they don't apply to telling our children about what it will be like when the new baby arrives.

Give simple information on a need-to-know basis
A preschooler needs to know that a baby is growing in mummy's tummy. The reason that he needs to know is because everyone else is talking about it, so it would be common courtesy to let him in on it.

Toddlers and preschoolers don't have any concept of six months, so just tell him it takes a very long time to grow a baby and it is growing very slowly.

Preschoolers need to know what is happening to *them*. So, as you get nearer to delivery, give him some idea of the plan to care for him while Mummy has the baby and Daddy will be away helping Mummy.

Deal in facts, not feelings. Let him have his own feelings. If he expresses feelings, respond then. Don't expect him to be joyful or sad or worried beforehand. Let him be.

Make your home safe for your baby
You need a toddler who can be annoyed without hitting, be excited without squealing, who can hug gently without squeezing juices out of your neck, who can obey simple instructions — particularly the 'leave it alone' sort — and can occupy himself quietly while being close to Mum but not on her lap.

It will never be easier than now to train these behaviours. They will ensure that you can trust your preschooler in the same room as the baby.

Your baby will not have to endure ear-splitting shrieks that cause her to levitate before she can crawl. Your preschooler will be able to give and receive affection from the baby without endangering the baby's life or your blood-pressure. You will be able to feed your baby while giving your preschooler full and positive attention.

Fairy tales are good
Have a lovely present 'from the baby' waiting in the baby's bassinet when the preschooler first arrives. It's like Santa Claus and the Easter Bunny. Our preschoolers recognize that it is important to parents that they believe that the baby bought it. They are happy to oblige us in our fantasy.

Don't tolerate ghastly behaviour
We tend to have a very strange explanation for unacceptable behaviour after the arrival — and by after the arrival I mean any time in the next twenty years — of a new family member.

'He's jealous.'

While it is true that there may well be feelings of enormous outrage and jealousy, it is not good for our child to express this through unacceptable behaviour. If we want our children to feel secure in our love and care, we must show them that the constancy and security of the basic household rules, such as:

- no hitting
- be gentle
- be kind

apply now just as much as they did a week ago, a month ago, or a year ago.

Happy parenting!

— *Essentially Food*

What is pocket money for?

OUR FIRST-BORN WAS ABOUT eighteen months old when my mother said to me 'Don't ask me about potty training because I was never any good at it.' There was enormous comfort in having such wonderfully lowered expectations upon me.

So when, about two months ago, 'The Editor' said 'Diane, how about an article on pocket money?' my first thought was 'I've never had a pocket money scheme that I was able to be consistent about or to sustain for very long. Don't ask me.' Upon reflection, however, I do know a lot about what pocket money works for and doesn't work for.

Pocket money is great for counting
Our children have all loved having money to count and money to store. They very sensibly refused to have anything to do with a money box that needed to be destroyed before you could get the money out. However, those with a removable 'plug' provided hours of entertainment. They loved organising the coins by type, they loved making piles of coins, (five cent coins are great for helping little fingers master co-ordination), they loved making piles that added up to a dollar or five or ten.

Pocket money is great for trade and exchange
Our children loved trading up their coinage. At this stage of

development, parents need to be well-equipped and readily available bankers. Open all hours. You never know when you are going to be bailed up with a child clutching ten warm, sweaty five cent coins and demanding, 'Please Mummy, or in our case, Daddy — I had played more than enough Monopoly to know that being banker was a tedious job — can I change this for a big coin?'

Even more exciting was The Advanced Game. This involved trading small notes for larger notes and was much more fun in the days of one and two dollar notes. The day you finally got a fifty dollar note was truly a great notch above any sibling achievement.

Pocket money is great for practising decision making
Whether you give your child fifty cents to spend at the dairy on sweets or fifteen dollars to spend in The Warehouse on a birthday present, they will have to confront all the difficult issues around what they want and what they can afford, what they are going to choose and what that will mean they won't be able to choose. These are difficult decisions for many children, but they are good practice for them.

I suggest you take along a folding armchair, a good book and a thermos of coffee. If your child has difficulty making this sort of decision, a sleeping bag may also be necessary. Good things take time, you know.

Pocket money is great for parents who find it hard to say 'no'
You know what it is like. You are at the supermarket or you are driving past the dairy and your child says, 'Mum, can I have a . . . ?' It is such a relief to be able to say to your pocket-moneyed child, 'Of course you can, my darling. Can you afford it?' Then all you have to do is remember, as soon as you get back home, is to say to your child 'I need you to pay me back now' and be sure to follow-up immediately. Remember, you do not offer credit on next week's allowance.

Pocket money is a big punishment for parents trying to sort out sibling issues
If you have ever struggled with the issues of how to treat your children equally and how you can make it clear to them that you are a fair

parent, pocket money can help you hone your skills or at least drive you to distraction. Does your child get pocket money according to age, need, grandparents' generosity, parents' means, parents' memory. If you have a spread-out family, with older children who begin sentences with 'In my day . . .', I have learned that the best way to work out your exchange rate is to tie pocket money to multiples of the CEI (current expensive ice-cream) Index.

Pocket money is great for keeping charitable trusts honest
At one stage, we instituted a pocket money system whereby Deborah got three dollars a week. One dollar was for spending, one dollar was for saving and one dollar was for giving to charity. When there was a worthy cause knocking on our door for a donation, Deborah would race to get involved. She would bale up the hapless collector and want details about how her contribution would be used and how much of it would be spent on administration.

Pocket money is no substitute for dealing with non-compliance
There is little point in setting up a list of ordinary household tasks and persuading your children that they really want to save up for 'something big'. It gets even harder for us when we decide that we will take off points for tasks not done, halve the reward for a task badly done, remove ten points for beating up your baby brother, even though that was not one of the tasks in the first place!

Beware of thinking that you can hold this system over your child's head like a Sword of Damocles. The parent who cautions 'Remember that you need to make your bed because you are saving for that fantastic Pokemon toy' is likely to get the retort 'I don't want that stupid old thing anyhow.'

Pocket money is great for highlighting the generation gap
In my day, we took twenty cents a week for school banking and were praised for this effort and encouraged to watch our savings grow. If we took a pile of coins to the bank, the teller smiled glowingly and willingly counted it out and helped us fill in our own deposit form and we felt important and grown-up.

When I recently took our twelve-year-old in with a bag of coins, the teller looked horrified, counted it out with enormous reluctance and then, completely ignoring my presence, asked my daughter if *she* would like her own EFTPOS card.

Pocket money is great for learning
By all means set up a pocket money system. Your child will learn many things. You will learn many, many things. They just may not be the things you expected.

— Essentially Food

After-school activities

The family rule

My parents came from Central Europe and the family rule was that every child learned the piano and then, as we nudged towards secondary school age, our father would choose an orchestral instrument appropriate to our inclinations. Practising between lessons was taken for granted, so we did.

This was a great system for me because I was both musical and sociable, so playing in school orchestras gave me enormous pleasure. It worked well for my sister for much the same reasons. Our tone-deaf brother diverted our father by becoming a New Zealand chess champion.

I do recall going to two ballet lessons but I failed the entry test for five-year-olds, which involved lying on the floor on my tummy and touching my heels to my head. Since I couldn't achieve this minimal flexibility, my life as a ballerina was over before it started.

Anything of an outdoor, athletic nature was an anathema to our parents but our school Physical Education programme was daily and thorough and we learned the rudiments of all the sports a Kiwi Kid needed.

The next generation

When our first two children were young — to my amazement they are now nudging thirty — we decided that one waited for a child to ask and then followed the child's inclination. By the time they were respectively, ten and eight, no one had asked and so we reverted to child-raising theory A from my childhood, 'It is the mark of any cultured family that every child learns the piano'.

I had retained the memories of my parents racing around half of Auckland to take us to the 'best' teachers and embarked on finding a piano teacher who lived within walking distance, with a view to getting on with the rest of my life and paying tuition fees as necessary.

My 'lazy parent' plot failed dismally. The teacher took an enormous liking to me and insisted that I attended each lesson. She also thought that it was enchanting that a brother and sister should learn together and set about encouraging them to play duets. Since they were not capable of sitting next to each other on a settee to watch TV without ensuing bloodshed, playing duets was not an asset to their musical careers. After two years I gave up the struggle.

It may be of interest to you to know that, when they were in their twenties, they berated me for not insisting that they learned for longer and forcing them — believe me, I tried — as they both would have, and I quote, 'liked to be much better at playing the piano.'

This only goes to prove something we all know, as a parent. Not only can you not win, you rarely get to choose which way you will lose.

Wise words from a principal
Three and a half years ago, we sat in a school hall to hear the school principal introduce a group of third formers to the school that they would be entering the following year. I was most impressed that, as part of her welcome, she said to the parents, 'Your daughters will have more extra-curricular opportunities available to them than they can possibly take up. It is your job as parents to help them choose and to make sure that they do not over-commit themselves.'

So many opportunities . . .
From Babygym and Singing Rainbows onwards, the sporting, cultural and social opportunities available to our toddlers, preschoolers and

school-age children are truly remarkable and there is enormous pressure on us, as parents, to enrol in as many as possible to make these opportunities available to our children. There is a fair degree of guilt-mongering in the question 'What after-school activities are your children doing this term?'

. . . so little time
I also believe that we often commit ourselves to each child's extra-curricular activities as if they were an only child. Thus, we over-commit our time and energy and often forget that, while one child is at their favourite after-school activity, we will have two other hot, grouchy, tired children to entertain.

While many of us have perfectly satisfactory homes to go to, we spend from three to six o'clock most weekday afternoons trying to run dressing rooms in the back of our cars, smorgasbords through car windows in car parks and homework sessions on the bare floor at the back of a noisy school hall.

We arrive home after dinnertime and then have to begin the gruelling feed, bath and bed routine and also have to fit in and supervise that dreaded thing called 'practice'. Weekdays can be a nightmare of one driver and three activities. Weekends may bring two shift-workers for some activities, but the ability to share things between two parents almost guarantees that all activities will be at opposite ends of the city.

Beware of success
If you do find activities that your children really enjoy and are successful at, the punishment will be in inverse proportion to their success. If they are really good, their coaches will need to work with them three nights a week and one long session in the weekend. If they get to representative level, you will enjoy the delights of 5.00 a.m. weekend starts to get to another city and will get familiar with many motels dotted around New Zealand.

You will also get to wash uniforms, sew labels on, make fundraising fudge and drive carloads of large sweaty boys or loud shrieking girls. Our last, apparently harmless, 'Oh Mum, can I enter a speech competition next holidays?' resulted in a three-night motel stay, much travelling, much sight-seeing to fill in the gaps between competition items, much supermarket-raiding at strange hours and an enormous amount of fun and companionship with other parents and children.

And if I had to do it all over again?
I would moan and grizzle just as much. I would probably still over-commit us all and advise other parents not to follow my example.

But I would have missed a great deal if I had never been to a jazz ballet concert of five-year-olds, a soccer game where they enthusiastically scored a magnificent goal at the wrong end, a judo competition where they fight like crazy on the mat and support each other tenderly before and afterwards.

I have shed sentimental tears at speech competitions, debates, and the marching-on of hundreds of diminutive gymnasts. I have sewn costumes when I don't know how to sew, painted faces to look gorgeous or ferocious, put hair in nets with so many pins that the child rattled and sufficient hair spray that the Laws of Gravity no longer applied.

I have cheered till I was hoarse and clapped till I have had 'ring-blisters'. I have exchanged looks of empathy and warmth and excitement with the many parents who have shared the same passion. And I have carried numerous exhausted troupers from car to bed.

What have I learned?
It is hard to get the right balance between the opportunities for parents and for children and the exhaustion and satisfaction that go with it. Trial and error shows that, by the time you have worked out the best plan for your family, your children will be out of school and finished with after-school activities. You will heave a sigh of relief but, strangely enough, you will look back on them as some of the best parenting times.

— *Essentially Food*

The rain dance

LIFE HAS BEEN EXTREMELY hectic lately and, in an attempt to put off what needed to be done, I had been reading through some old articles that I wrote when Deborah, now seventeen, was nine.

This one particularly appealed to me, in the midst of turmoil, as it reminded me of two wonderful long weekends that I have spent at silent retreats — and how much I could do with one right now!

Peace of mind
From the day I developed speech, I have rarely been silent. I remember my parents despairingly describing my speaking as 'like a waterfall'. Our long-distance journeys were punctuated with heartfelt pleas of 'Couldn't you please be silent for just five minutes.'

The Universe got even on this one. We are blessed with a child whose verbal capacity is formidable. These days I often hear my parents' pleas coming out of *my* mouth.

My school reports always included 'Diane talks far too much.' Or, more pointedly, 'If Diane could only stop talking for a short amount of time, she might learn something.' I have eventually got even on that one. As a professional speaker, I am now *paid* to talk far too much!

You can imagine the merriment and disbelief from friends and family when I announced that I was going on a three-day silent retreat.

Frankly, no one thought that I could see it through. I had a few doubts myself. Would I be unable to contain myself and have to burst out with 'Have you heard the story of the . . . ?' Could I resist a simple 'How are you going?' when I passed someone in the corridor? What if I sang in the shower? Or giggled? Or laughed out loud?

To my initial amazement and eventual delight, I found the whole experience profoundly moving, excellent for my soul and one that I am eager to repeat. Once I learned to slow down and listen to the silence, I heard bees and cicadas; I felt the differences of the grass I walked on and the grain of the timber and the concrete of the path. I noticed leaves and flowers and the taste of food. I became temporarily vegetarian when I heard lambs 'baa' and cows 'moo'.

In my three days of thoughtfulness I had much time to ponder about the busyness of our lives, and the lives of our children. We sacrifice peace of mind and peace of spirit to the worship of fitting as much as we can into each day. If we don't think we are sufficiently efficient, we try to fix it with time management, list making, grouping tasks together and learning to relax deeply so you can pack a half-hour rest into five minutes in order to return refreshed to enter the craziness once more.

And what did I do with all this when I returned to the Real World called Home? I have tried to stay aware of the moment. I have become increasingly aware that, as we rush from one activity to the next, we have little time to savour what is happening. We are either rehashing the past or planning the future.

You may recall the massive downpour a few weeks ago. The skies emptied onto our garden. Deborah, a typical child of our times, announced, 'It's raining. Can I watch *Hook*?' Enthused by my new experience of the simple things in life, I abhorred the use of an electronic medium that encourages brainless passivity. I opted for craziness instead.

'Why don't you run around in the rain,' I suggested. She looked at me as if I had lost my marbles but quickly vanished to do an improvised Rain Dance — presumably to encourage its continuation. She progressed to stamping in puddles and finally testing the torrents in the gutter.

No! I did not feel moved to join her. I was, however, glad that a child who has been 'car-pooled' all her life and is a proficient user of an electric garage door opener had, for the first time in her nine years of life, pranced around in the rain.

I doubt that there is a profound moral to this story. However, there is none so passionate as the 'new discoverer' and so I am happy to proclaim, 'Silence is Great'.

So I would encourage us all to try a little silence, a little listening to the birds singing, and maybe gaze at the odd flower. Give your children some natural experiences and some time to stand and stare — and to wonder.

The sequel

You may like a follow-up on the previous event, when Deborah pranced around in the rain and I congratulated myself on the return to the good and simple things in life.

When the next downpour came about a fortnight later, Deborah begged, 'Can I go out in the rain again, Mummy? It's the best thing I have ever done in my whole life.' My feeling of Earth-Mother-smugness was interrupted three minutes later by ear-splitting shrieks. Deborah had been stung by a wet wasp. She followed up with a very bad cold!

— Essentially Food

You can't go out looking like that!

WHEN WILL OUR CHILDREN learn to dress decently? How many times will we have to say, 'You can't go out looking like that!' before our children grow up? Alternatively, how long till they move to another city so we won't have to watch and cringe?

There seems to be such a short time between arguing with our four-year-old who is promising not to get pneumonia, 'You can't go outside in a T-shirt when there is a frost', and arguing with our fourteen year old, 'You cannot possibly go to Grandpa's eightieth birthday with your midriff hanging out and your skirt shorter than your eyelashes.'

While raising two teenage girls, I have been required to choose between fashion, taste, decency and safety many times. I have been guilty of yelling, 'How come we are all ready to go and you haven't even started', when I seriously misunderstood the time and effort involved in achieving a particular look. And I strongly recommend that you consider carefully before declaring 'Your hair needs a good brush.' I now know that it takes hours to get that bird-nest creation perfect.

Vernon has been guilty of wandering in with the laundry basket asking in bewildered tones, 'We all seem to have reasonable eyesight. Who is wearing eye patches in various colours in this household?'

He is now better informed about the mysteries of G-strings.

I now know that there is a magic word that we can teach our children in their early years. Later, we will be able to use it to make a point about their clothing rather than attack the ego or taste of the budding fashion aficionado.

When Deborah was about three, we introduced her to the word 'appropriate'. She could barely pronounce it, but she rapidly learned that the world could be divided into two categories — appropriate and inappropriate. Whether it was certain words, certain deeds or certain clothes, she seemed to gain enormous satisfaction as the question rolled off her tongue, 'Mummy, is that appropriate?' And we had a wonderful weapon of reprimand. 'Deborah! That behaviour is completely inappropriate.'

It was such a useful adjective to shortcut debates about why Anglo-Saxon as a second language seemed to be used freely in the playground but unacceptable in the kitchen. 'That language is just not appropriate for my ears!'

After many a false start, we found that what to wear — based on the appropriateness of the occasion — was a much better arbiter than parental or teenage taste. We also developed a system that worked for deciding *who* would designate what was or wasn't appropriate.

If the invitation came from an adult, the adults of our household had a say in what was or was not suitable to wear. If the invitation came from a peer, the teen decided what was appropriate to wear. After all, she was the one who had done hours of telephone investigative research into what everyone else was wearing, so it was likely that she would know what was — dare I say — appropriate.

We also discovered another good idea. When we were going into our children's territories such as school functions, sports functions, jazz ballet recitals or speech competitions, we would ask them before we chose our clothing, 'Would this be appropriate?'

At least it saved us from having an irate teen yell at us, 'You can't possibly go out looking like that!'

— Essentially Food

Family meals — heaven or hell?

MANY OF US HARK BACK to a distant memory. It may be of our family, it may be of someone else's family, it may be of a mythical and entirely unreal Television Family. It is of a family sitting around the meal table, everyone cheerful, co-operative children — hands washed, faces clean, hair tied back — who have, no doubt, taken part in meal preparation and setting the table, positive talk only with everyone taking turns and listening respectfully, appreciation expressed for the delightful food, a heart-warming atmosphere of closeness, family unity and willing helpers to clean up.

There is an appropriate teenage response to this mirage, to be uttered with scornful sarcasm. 'Yeah, right.'

As if we, as parents, do not have enough guilt heaped upon us about the busyness of our lives and the damage that fragmented families must endure, we are now being told that we can do restorative work by ensuring that the family sits down to a meal together and has 'quality time'. 'Yeah, right.'

Now, we mums have done our bit towards the mythical family meal. We have organised, shopped, prepared food, set beautiful tables, arranged plates appealingly, had all the kids ready on time, forced Dad home early from the office, switched off the TV, put on the answer phone, hidden the mobiles in the fishbowl — but does that mean that it will take less than thirty seconds for the first whine and less than three minutes for the first tantrum? Not on your nelly!

Yes! It is lovely when we can all sit down together and enjoy each other's company around a family mealtime. But if you are looking for a family meal around the dining room table as the only way to forge a strong family, forget it.

In the year 2003, families eat in varied places and at various times and all of them can be good for families and good for individuals, if we make them so. These days, our children are expected to know the rules and customs for eating in a wide variety of circumstances and a wide variety of food.

They know that some meals involve fingers, some involve cutlery and some involve chopsticks. Some meals are children only, some are just with Mum and some are with Mum and Dad. Some are with a tiny family only and some are with an extended family and friends. Some are for nutrition only, some are for catching up on news and some are had on the run in the back of the car between swimming and ballet.

We have taught our children to eat with cutlery, which cutlery is used for what purpose, to eat soup without slurping, what serviettes are for and which sort of glasses are used for which sort of drink. Our children have taught us how to order Japanese food, what are the best combinations to get at a drive-through and how to stack an eat-all-you-can-get-in-for-one-price pita pocket to maximum advantage.

A few weeks ago, Vernon and I had a rare moment on our own and decided on designer hamburgers at a place our daughter has frequently raved about. We were the oldest people in the hamburger café by at least thirty-five years. We were presented with this amazing assortment of very slippery meats and slidey vegetables, surrounded with an array of wonderful, drippy sauces and all looking harmless enough encompassed by two halves of a very large hamburger bun.

All went well until we tilted them in order to begin eating. Clearly we did not know about the highly skilled 'grip and turn' required to eat-without-wearing such food. By the time we had finished, we and our surroundings looked much as if two overgrown toddlers had been left alone for too long with bowls of spaghetti and tomato sauce.

The following week we persuaded out daughter to come and teach us the correct etiquette and technique required for this form of dining. Pretty soon we will be skilled enough so that she can eat with us in public. It is not all one-way traffic when it comes to learning how to eat properly.

There are lots of ways in which we have eaten together and combined nutrition, conversation and togetherness. We have had many meals around the family dining table with three generations and lots of tradition and memories. We have had some of our best conversations with our children when we have taken them individually on a coffee, breakfast or lunch 'date'.

My particular favourite traditional family meal in our household has been on Sunday nights when there was a smorgasbord of all available food put out on the table. The grown-ups sat at the table, the children — that is anyone who was not a parent — sat or lay around a tablecloth on the floor. People hopped up and helped themselves to food whenever they felt like it. Light and easy programmes were chosen on the TV. Conversations happened in ad breaks and sometimes became so interesting we forgot that the programme had started up again.

So let's acknowledge that our children are marvellous in the way in which they can know the rules and cope with the many different ways of eating that are required of them these days.

If you wish to add 'whole family dining in harmony together' to the ways in which your family eats, here are some ideas that may help it work.

Don't bring starving children to the meal table
If dinner is not at their 'tummy hungry' time, give them a decent snack beforehand and regard anything eaten at the table as a bonus.

Split up the battlers
If children are inclined to fight with each other, place a large peace-loving adult between them. Avoid putting the fussy, squeamish child opposite the one who eats like a concrete mixer with his mouth wide open.

Don't comment on what anyone has or hasn't eaten
Forget about nutrition for this meal. Family harmony is much more important.

Don't allow bad behaviour
The most important thing is not that the numbers at the table stay the same for the entire meal. You are better off to send a badly behaved child to his room until he has changed his mind and decided to act appropriately, rather than all endure the growling and threaten-ing of reprimands.

Allow them to go and return
Some of our best and longest meals have been when we have allowed our children to leave as soon as they have had enough main course and return for dessert. After such a break they have often returned, hooked into the adult conversation and stayed so polite, friendly and involved, that their parents never noticed how far beyond bed-time it was!

— Essentially Food

Show some respect

IN AUGUST LAST YEAR, we were flying back to New Zealand from Singapore. I was handed a copy of the local newspaper and turned to a page that had questions about parenting. There was a question there about a four-year-old boy who was reluctant to have his teeth cleaned each night.

The answer intrigued me because it was so far removed from our Western way of offering inducements or punishments. The Singaporean parenting expert recommended that the parent should quietly and firmly insist, saying 'I wouldn't be fulfilling my responsibility as a parent if I let you neglect your teeth and not take good care of them by brushing them.'

I was entranced by this reply. It allowed no leeway — the child was definitely going to get his teeth brushed. It was so respectful of the child. It changed the issue from power and control, or praise and punishment, to respect for the responsibilities of a parent and respect for the position of the child. Even if the parent had to pin the child down and forcibly brush his teeth, it was still done through respect and responsibility.

We are often disrespectful
It set me to thinking about the times we are often disrespectful of the integrity of our children. One day, a few summers ago, I was sitting

on Waiwera beach and saw virtually simultaneously, two ways of introducing a toddler to waves. Four-inch waves that is!

In the first family group, the dad was carrying the toddler in his arms. The deeper they got, the closer the toddler got to the water, the more the toddler screamed. He was clearly terrified but the dad was persisting on the basis that once the toddler was in the water he would love it and have a great time. Mum was walking alongside Dad encouraging their child that he really was having a good time, patting his back and sprinkling water on his flailing legs.

In the second family group, the parents were sitting on the beach about ten feet from the water's edge, relaxed and alert. Their toddler was running after the waves as they receded and then hot-footing it up the beach as the waves came in. With each successive wave, he got closer and closer to getting in and eventually plumped himself onto the sand and let the water run over his legs. There were a lot of delighted shrieks to be heard over the waves.

The second set of parents respected their child's ability to gradually approach the water at his own pace and saw their job as guarding their toddler's safety.

Just try it — you'll like it

Often, we put a plateful of food in front of our child, who wrinkles up his nose and says, 'I don't like that.' Now I can't comment about you, but I do know that my most likely response would be, 'Just try it. I'm sure that you'll like it.'

How disrespectful is that! We are very sensibly designed to assess food by its appearance and smell before we actually put it into our mouths. If we were dishing up for an adult guest, we might respectfully ask, 'Is there anything you don't particularly like?' With our own children, we over-ride the information they have already gleaned through *their* eyes and *their* nose and insist, despite all evidence to the contrary, that *their* assessment is wrong. Surely, it would be much more respectful to say, 'I know you don't like the look or smell of that, but how about giving your tastebuds a chance to form an opinion?'

Now I am not suggesting that you run an all day smorgasbord to meet your children's whims. I do recommend, however, that you respect your child's assessment that it is not a flavour/texture that appeals to him.

I'm cold — you need a jacket

How often do we get into arguments with our children about their body temperature. We insist that they are cold. They insist that they are not. We have a fair idea of the weather forecast. They have a fair idea about current kid-fashion. We don't want them to get wet and then get ill. They think that they can promise not to get ill and uphold that promise. And they know that they are waterproof!

Rather than argue, I have found it is more respectful — and definitely more effective — to say, 'I am freezing, please put on a jacket.' They look puzzled, but they usually comply. If you encounter resistance, another way that I have found useful is to say, 'I am freezing. I would feel so much better if I knew you had your jacket in your school bag.'

That enables them to swagger out the door dressed for the tropics and still have the means, when the goosebumps are taller than the hair-spikes, of making their *own* decision to put on their jacket.

I'm not paying for that

At the beginning of summer, I went with Deborah (then seventeen) on a swimsuit hunt. She emerged from the changing room looking absolutely ravishing in what, to my parental eye, looked like three extremely small isosceles triangles. I choked back my usual parental rave, such as 'Are you crazy? There's no way you can even be thinking I would buy that for you. It is completely unacceptable. Why did you even bother to try it on?'

Instead, I went for respecting her integrity while guarding her safety. 'Darling, you look absolutely stunning in that. The problem is that I could only cope with your wearing that in the bathroom. Probably with the door shut and the lights off.' Amazingly, she went and chose something more in line with what the parental blood-pressure could handle.

So, parents, let's try some of those comments again. Let's try to show our children a little respect. Who knows? We may even get some back!

— *Essentially Food*

C U L8R! GR8!

I HAVE ALWAYS ENJOYED trying to make out what number plates are trying to say. AV8OR lives in our area and IDIG4U travels through occasionally. Little did I realise that the introduction of 'message' number plates was sent to induct the parental generation into the world of modern communication.

I am referring to the cellphone — an amazing device which has changed teen communication and parental supervision for ever.

Some of you will be old enough to remember how we used to make arrangements to meet our school friends in the holidays. (I am not going to even attempt to explain to our teens that holidays were the only time we went to the pictures!)

Our arrangements went something like this. 'Mum! I'm meeting Elizabeth outside Whitcombe's at 1.30 and then we are going to the two o'clocks. [That was the only option — apart from the eleven o'clocks!] I'll be home on the five o'clock bus.'

Our parents knew where we were planning to be, when we were planning to be there and when we were planning to return home. They had very simple decisions to make:

Yes, you can or No, you can't.

Here is the money or Have you got enough left in your purse?

It is very hard not to feel a twinge of envy for the good old days when children asked permission, parents knew exactly where they were and money could only be got out of the bank by parents during working hours.

Today, the arrangements, or lack thereof, are more likely to proceed like this.

Teen: I'm meeting up with my friends tomorrow.
Mum: Which friends?
Teen: I don't know yet. Depends who's there.
Mum: There. Where?
Teen: I don't know yet.
Mum: What time do you think you're going?
Teen: I don't know yet.

I must point out that this is not a conversation with a rebellious, difficult or secretive teen. This is a typical conversation with a co-operative one who is genuinely trying to keep her parents informed. This is the conversation with a teen who has been part of a fixed arrangement. 'Let's hang out tomorrow.' The teen is giving the parent as much information as she has, as soon as she has it!

Tomorrow begins as each individual teen wakes at their own individual time. They begin texting each other 'WHERE R U' and if more than one has replied 'NWMRKT' — that's *Newmarket,* in case you don't parent in Auckland — the location of the gathering has been established. Armed with this piece of geography, your teen will approach and give you *full information* to date. 'We are all going to Newmarket.'

Don't bother asking 'What time?' or 'Whereabouts in Newmarket?' or 'What are you going to do there?' All will be revealed in good time. The information is not yet available.

After much changing of clothing — we looked in our cupboard and decided what to wear: they look at their floor and try on several combinations until more-or-less satisfied — the look is established and the teen gets on the bus and heads towards the broadly-defined destination. Back to texting 'WHERE R U'.

Several teen texters will now be walking along a crowded footpath together. You can recognise them because they form a footpath traffic hazard with their eyes firmly focused downwards and their thumbs working at a speed that was, in a previous lifetime, matched only by knitting grandmothers! Their activity will occasionally be punctuated by a call of 'Hey! Cal is joining us later!'

It doesn't matter what time your bus gets in or your Mum is free to give you a lift. All you have to do is text and U CN find out where YR FRNDS R. If enough of your friends have decided what to do, you can join in when you get there. Once the decision is made, teens can call their parents to tell them what they are doing, where and with whom.

In one sense, the advertisements are correct. If your child has a cellphone, you will know where they are and who they are with. The problem is that — should you wish to be a responsible parent who seeks information and then, after careful consideration, gives permission — you need to understand that you can only give permission retrospectively and you are supposed to give permission instantly. Should you require more details or hesitate fractionally before giving permission, you are likely to have an apologetic teen saying, 'Sorry Mum. Phone's running out. Talk to you later.'

The beauty of the cellphone — say the ads — is that your teen never has to stand around in dark and dangerous places waiting to be picked up. Whenever it looks like the group is going to disperse, your teen can phone for a lift.

'Hey, Mum. I'm ready.'

'I'll be there as soon as I can. It will probably take me twenty minutes to get to Newmarket.'

'No Mum! We bussed to Ponsonby!'

'But that's thirty minutes away! Why didn't you tell me?'

'My phone had run out. Cal's is running out now too. Bye Mum. Thanks Mum. Love you Mum.'

To give responsible teens all credit, they will stay in safe clusters until they are picked up. Once in the car, your teen will have to text her friends to rehash today and to work out tomorrow.

How come her phone had run out before but now works perfectly? I don't quite understand. I am still getting to grips with the teen cellphone culture. I believe that it has something to do with power!

C U L8R
GD LCK WTH YR PARNTNG!

— *Essentially Food*

littlies™

free monthly mag
for practical parenting!

- quality parenting information
- credible expert panel
- 10 editions a year
- regular dad's section
- audited 70,000+ copies
- and it's FREE to you!

6 months + up to five

www.littlies.co.nz